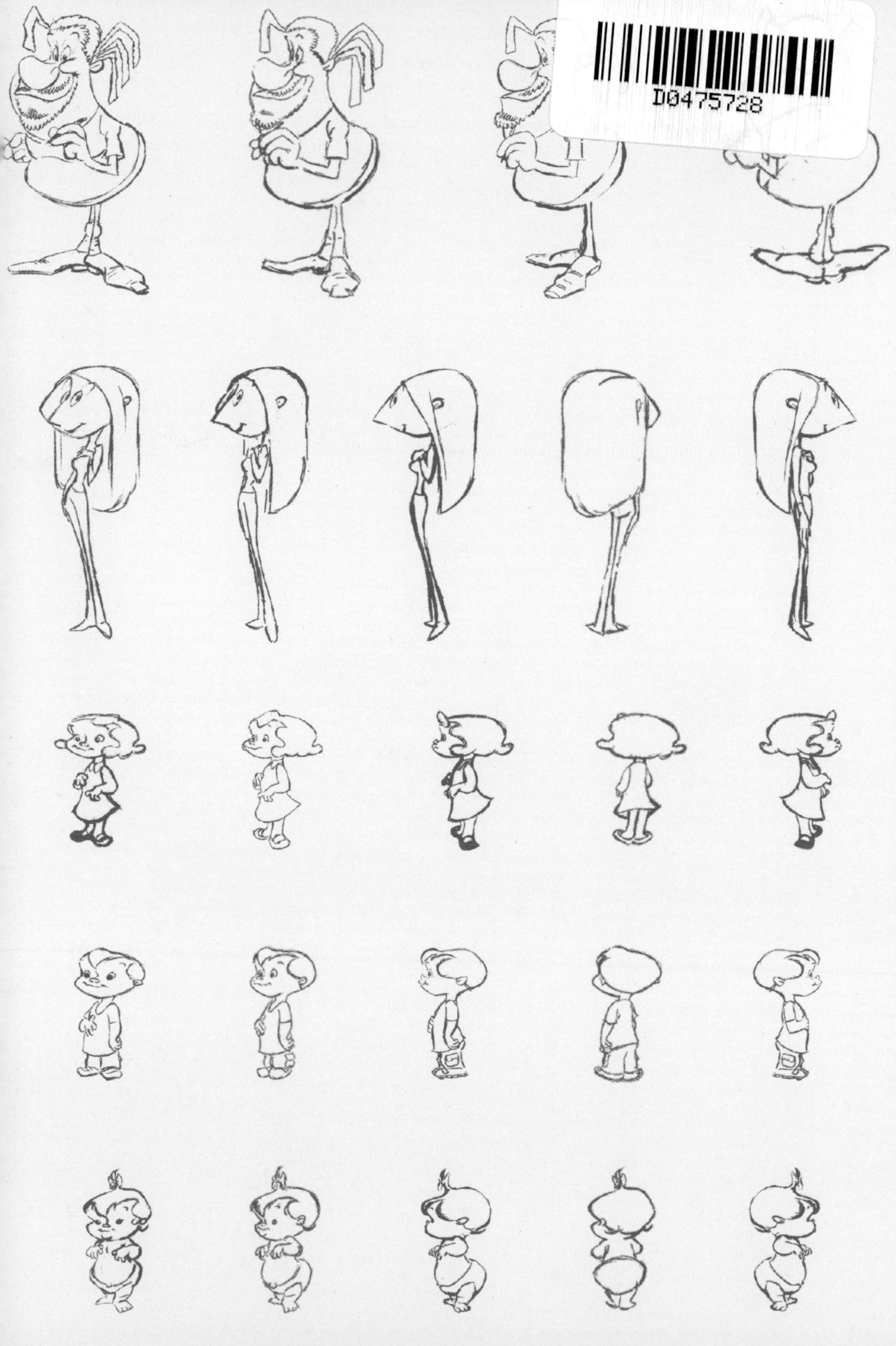

The Bakers™

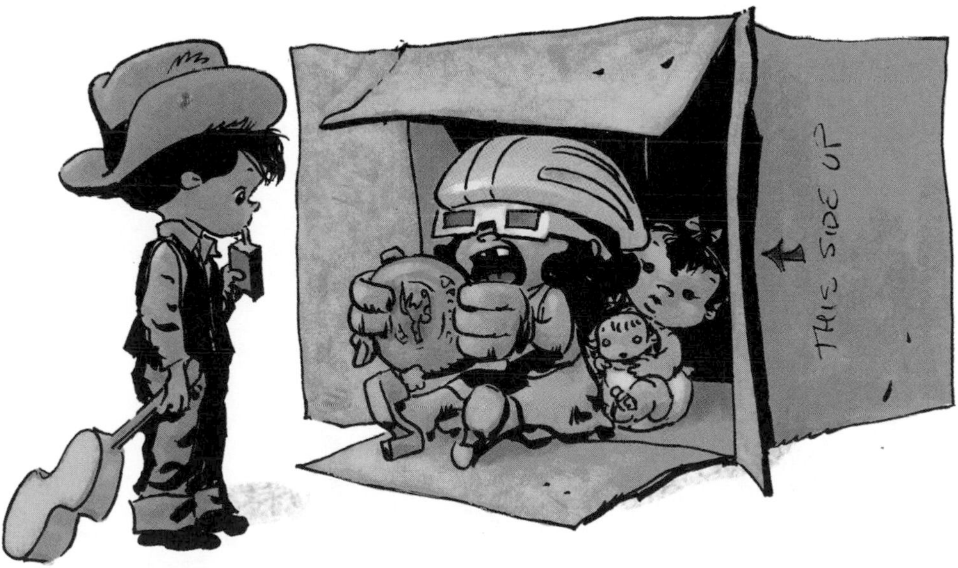
THIS SIDE UP

"Get out of the way!"

KYLE BAKER

Kyle Baker

The Bakers™

BABIES AND KITTENS

IMAGE COMICS

BERKELEY, CALIFORNIA, 2007

THE BAKERS:
BABIES AND KITTENS

copyright 2007 by Kyle Baker

All rights reserved, including the right to reproduce this book or portions thereof in any form whatsoever.

Published by

IMAGE COMICS

Erik Larsen - Publisher ~ Todd McFarlane - President ~ Marc Silvestri - CEO ~ Jim Valentino - Vice-President
Eric Stephenson - Executive Director ~ Joe Keatinge - PR & Marketing Coordinator ~ Thao Le - Accounting
Branwyn Bigglestone - Accounting ~ Traci Hui - Traffic Manager ~ Allen Hui ~ Production Manager
Jonathan Chan ~ Production Artist ~ Drew Gill ~ Production Artist

WWW.IMAGECOMICS.COM

1942 University Avenue, Suite 305, Berkeley, California 94704

VISIT WWW.KYLEBAKER.COM

ISBN: 978-1-58240-813-2

First Printing 2007

10 9 8 7 6 5 4 3 2 1

Printed in China

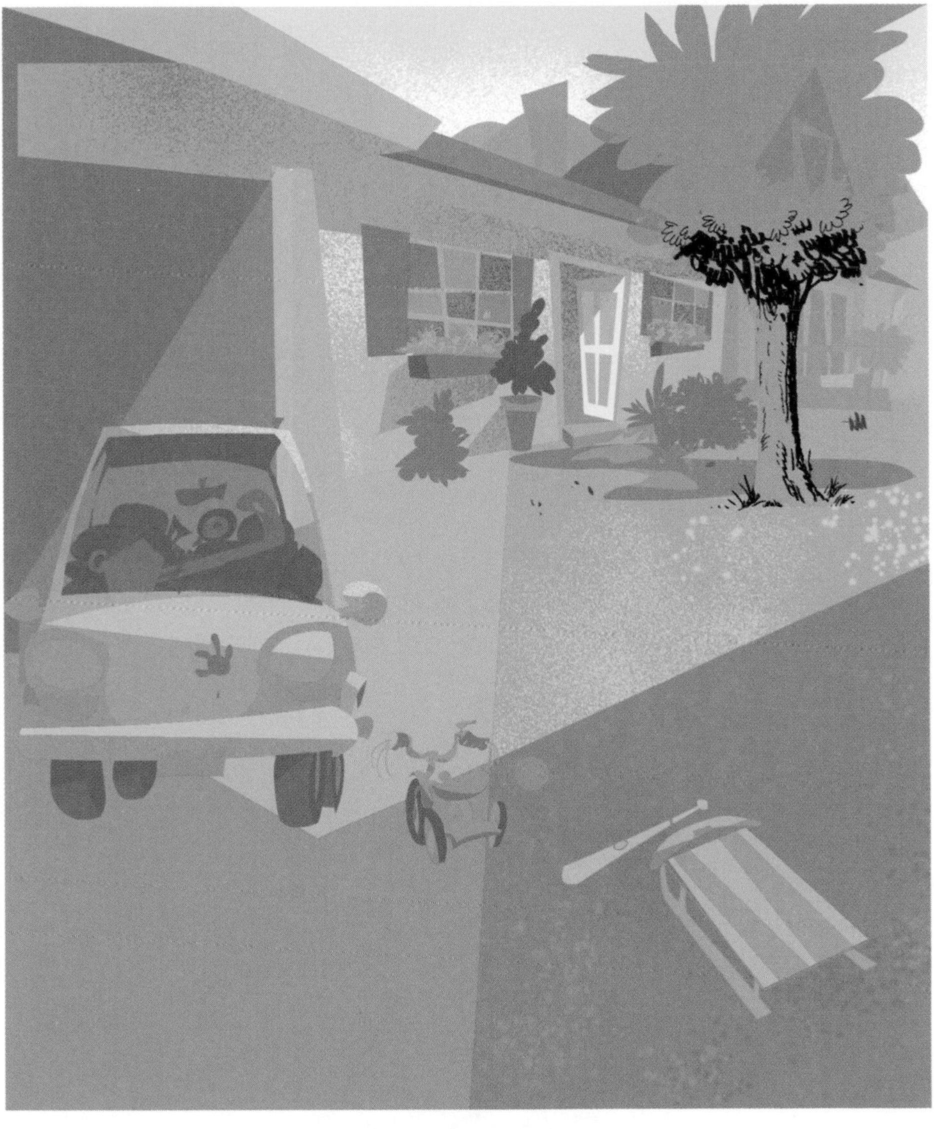

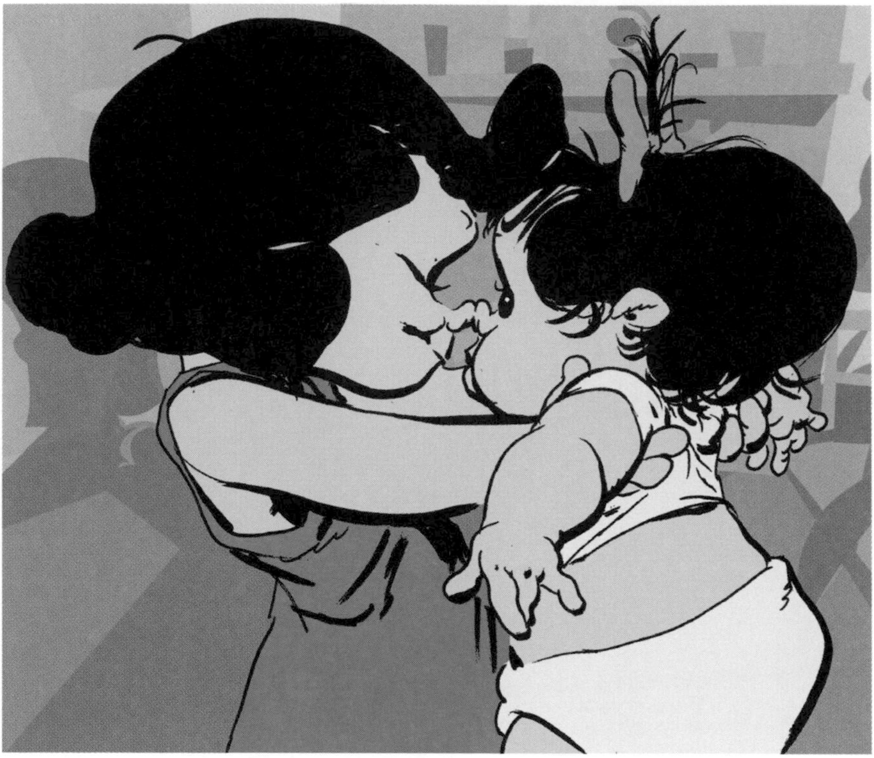

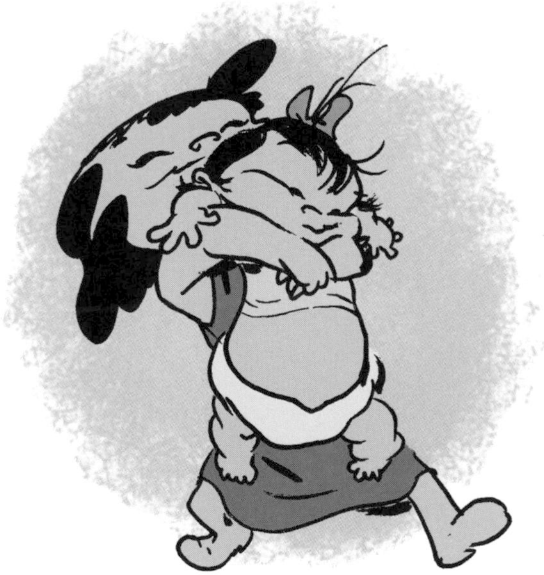

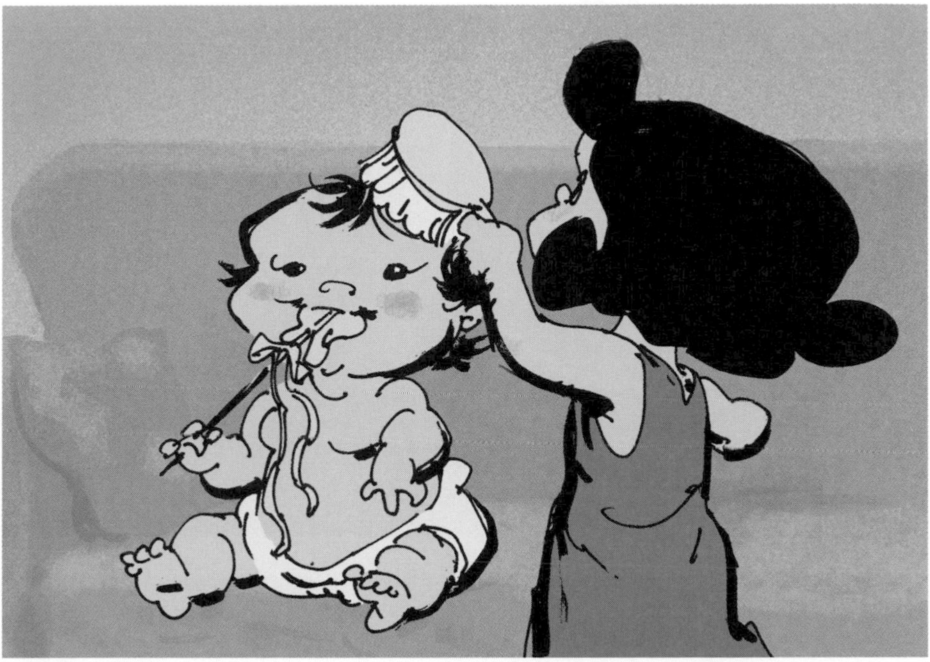

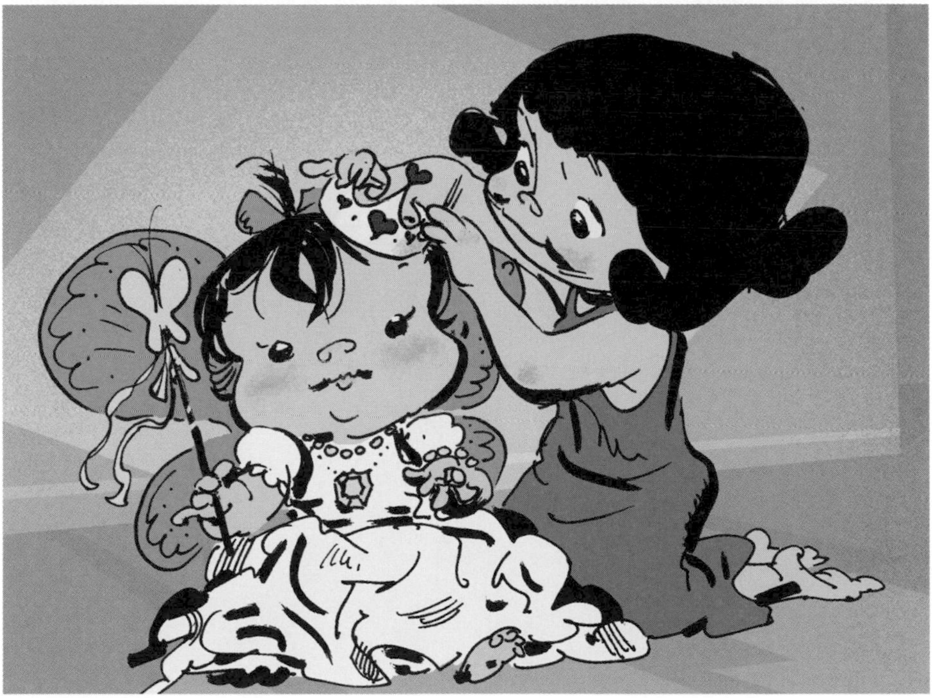

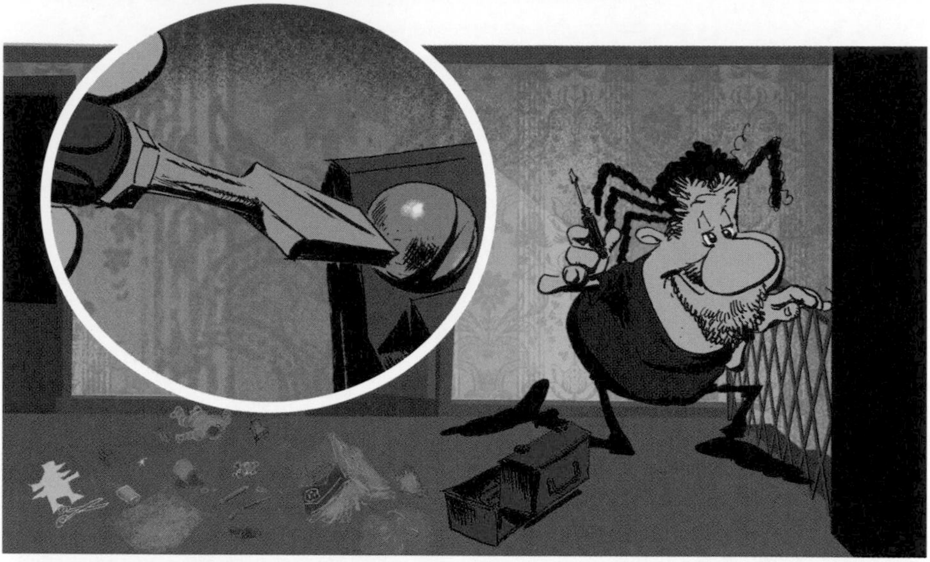

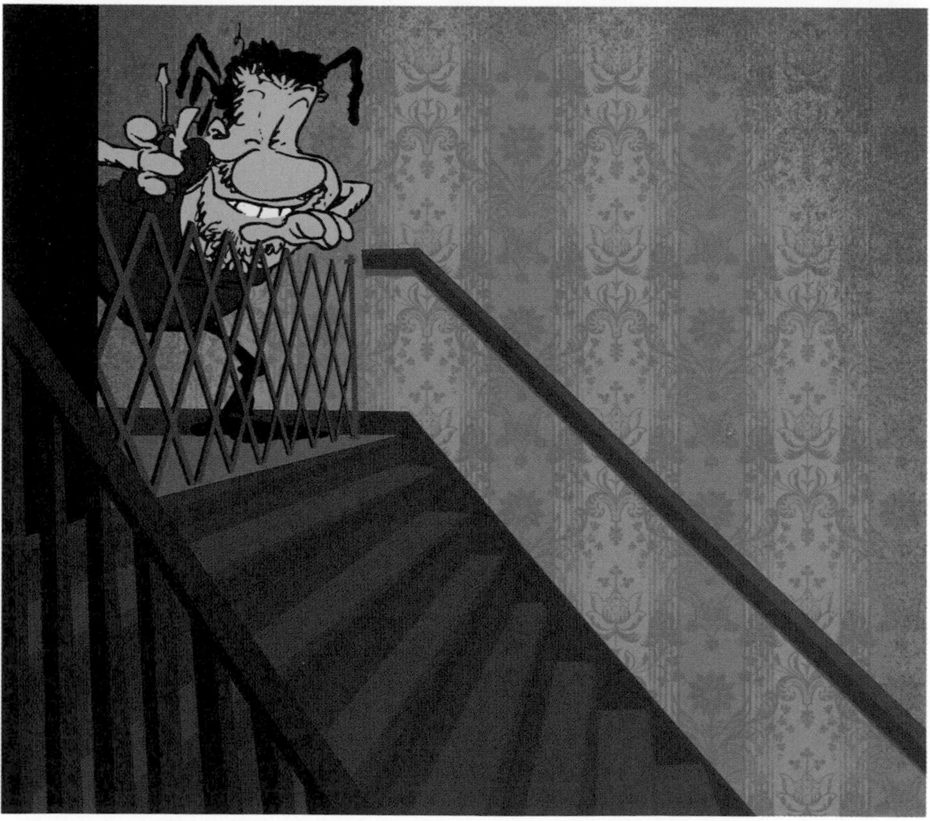

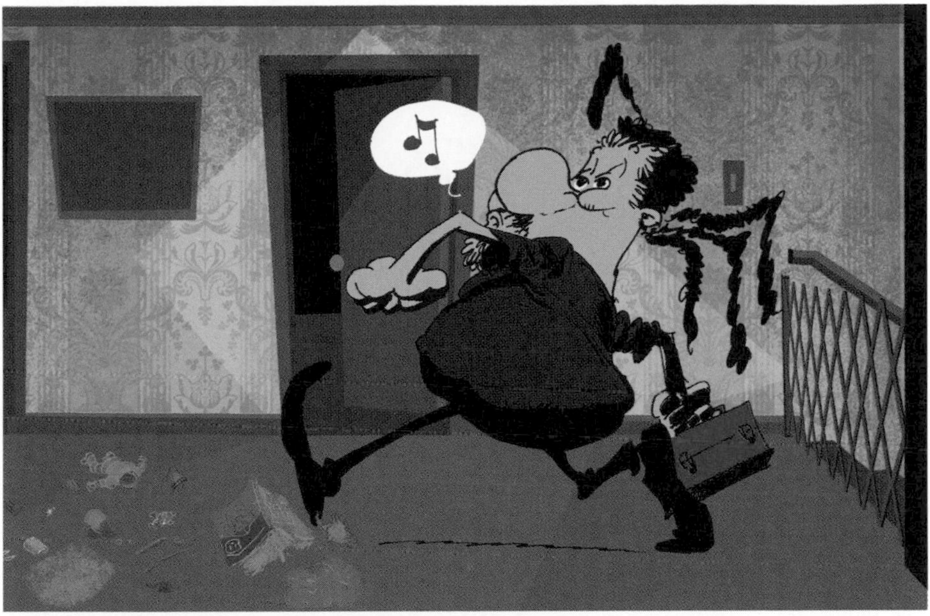

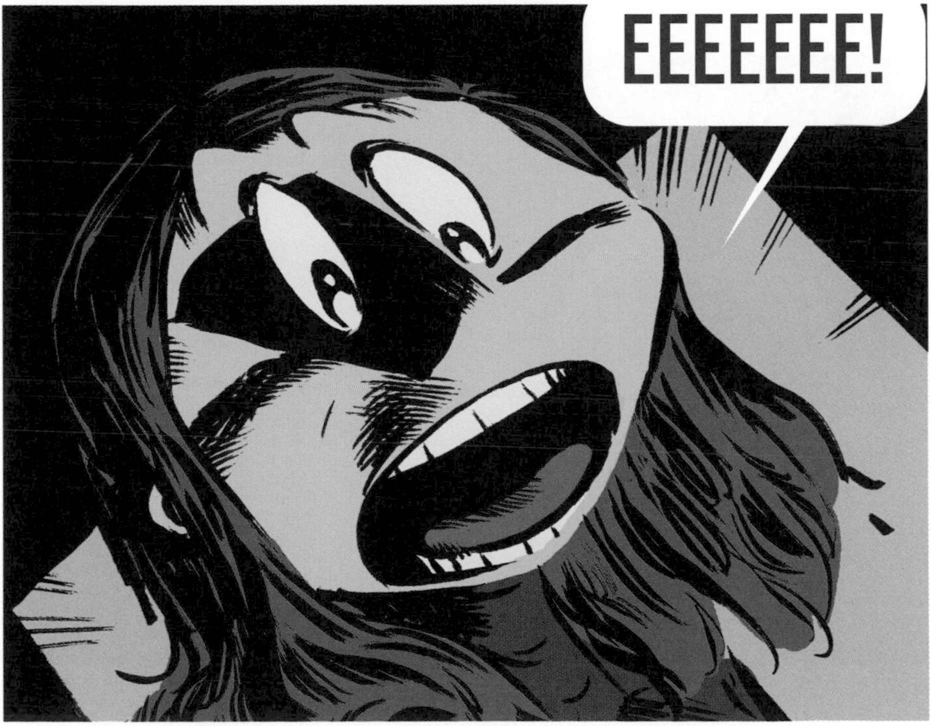
EEEEEEE!

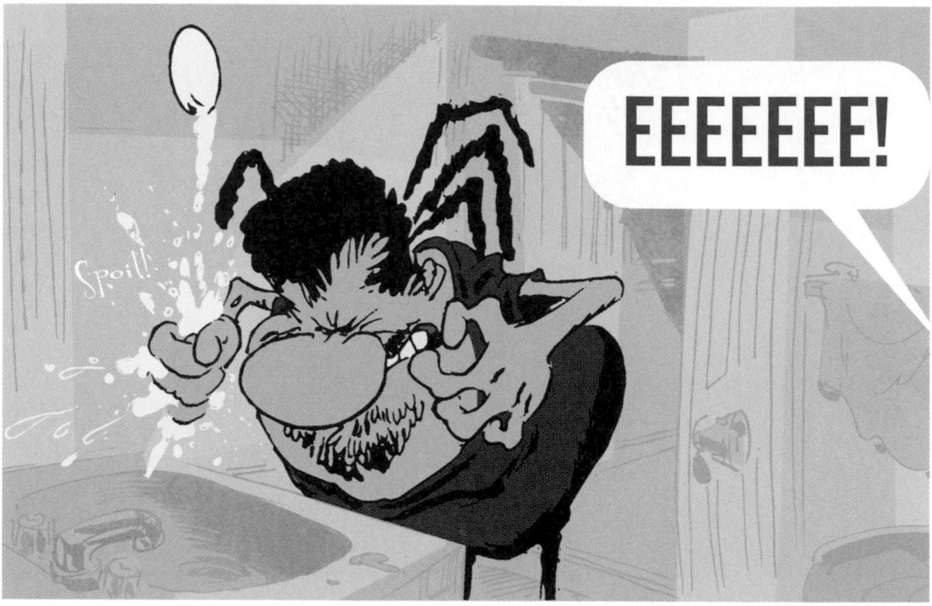
Spoil!
EEEEEEE!

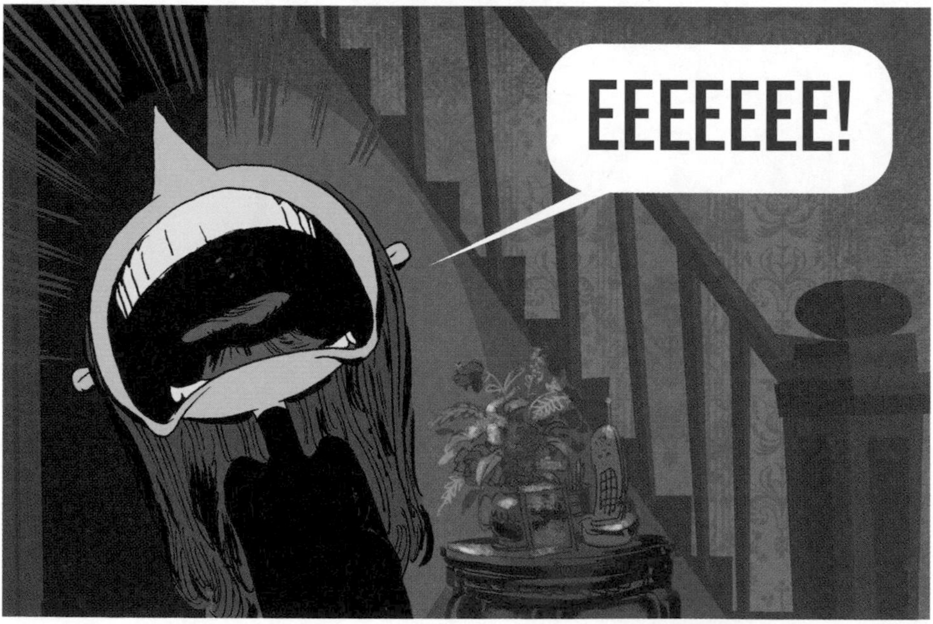
EEEEEEE!

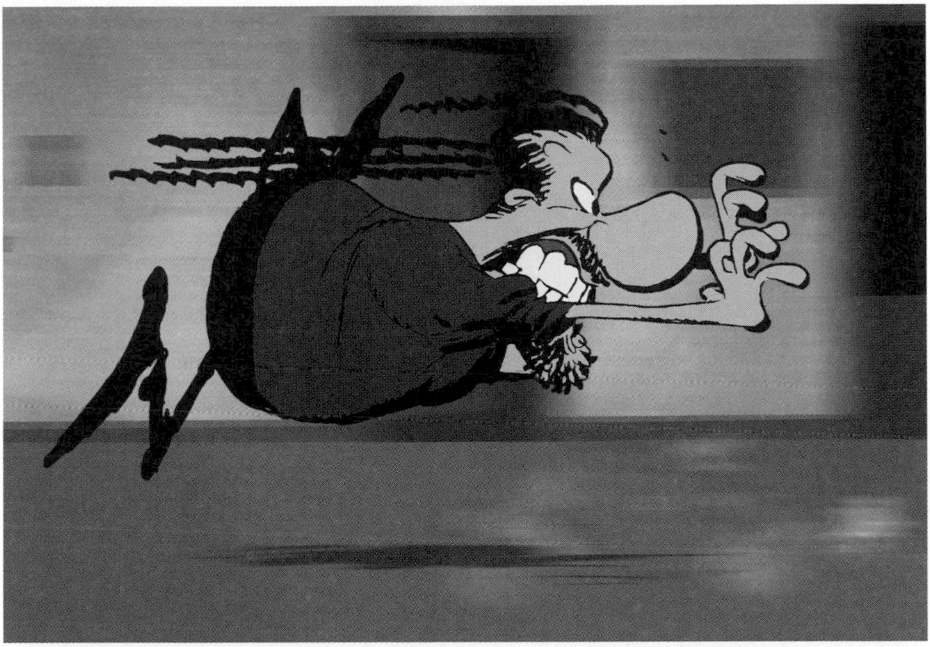

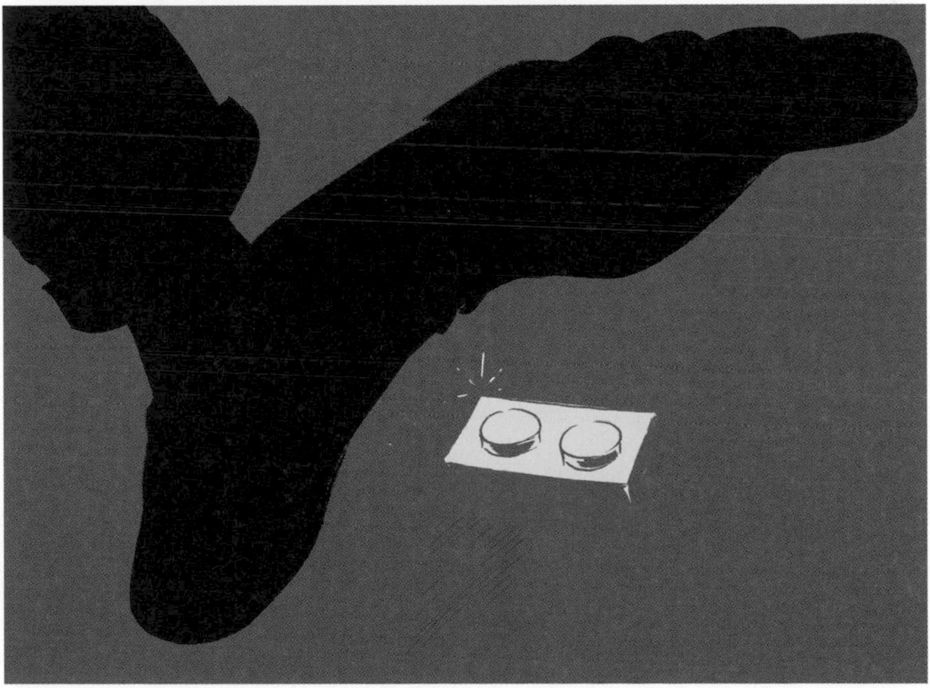

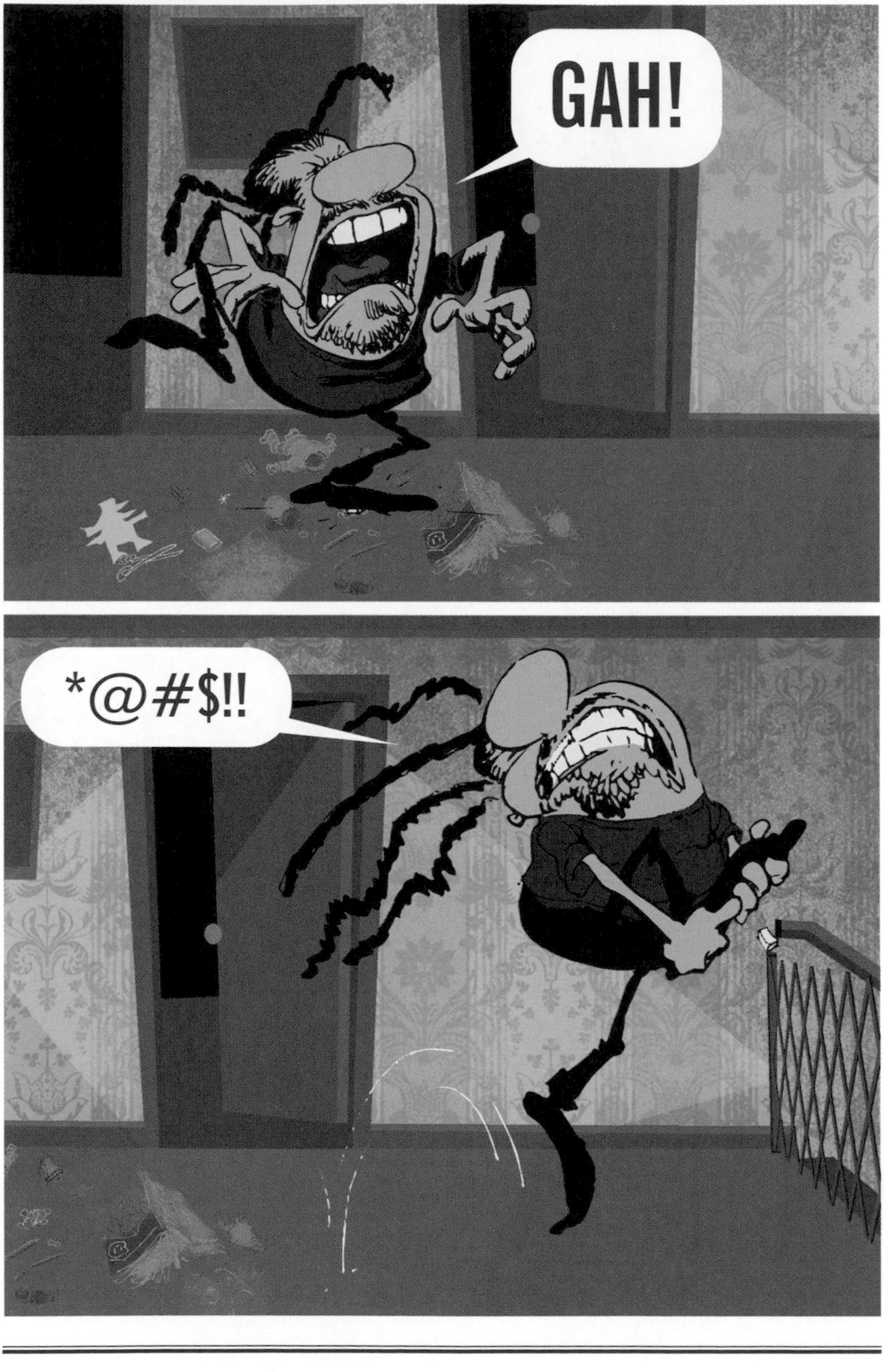
GAH!
*@#$!!

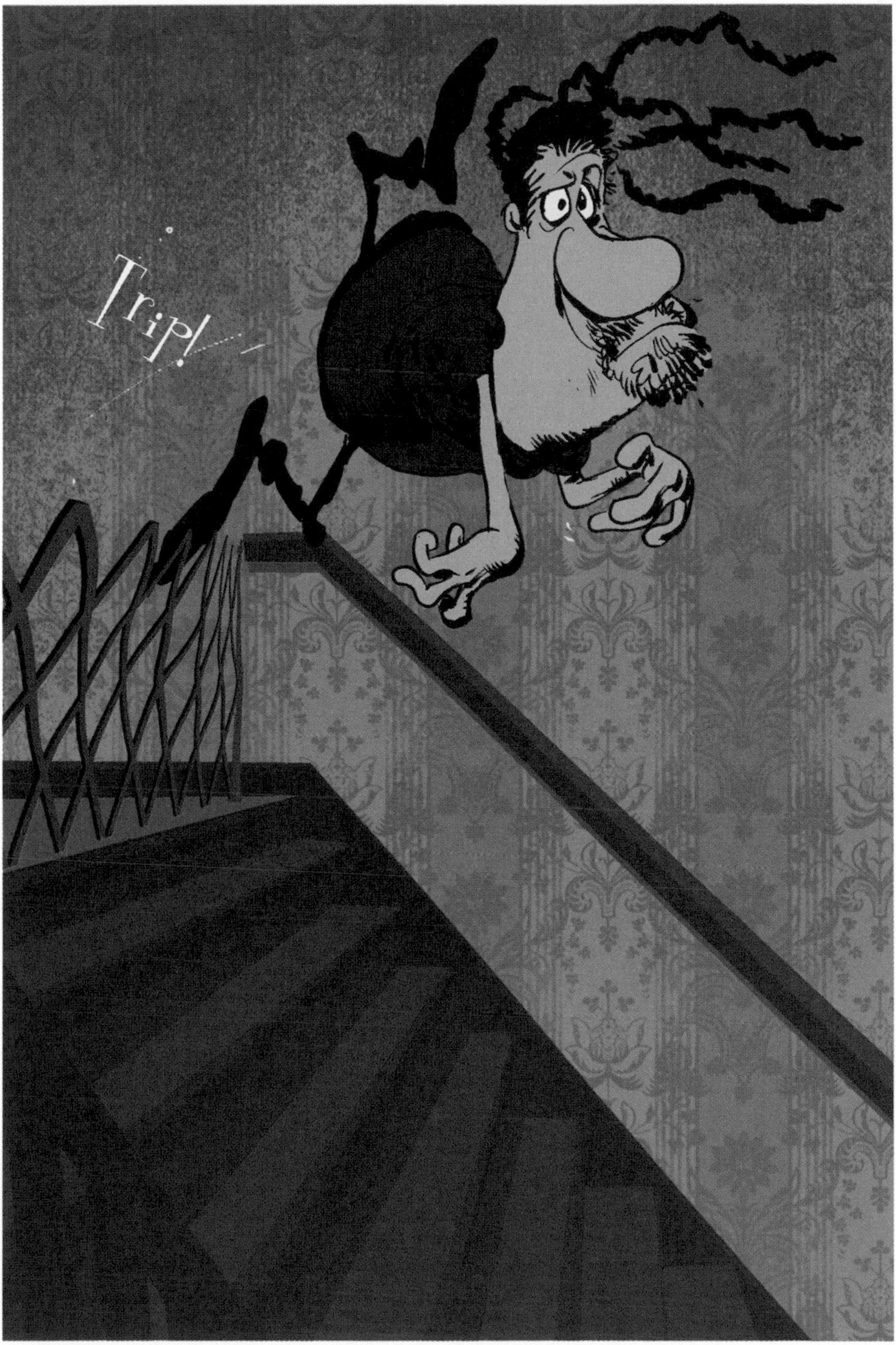
Trip!

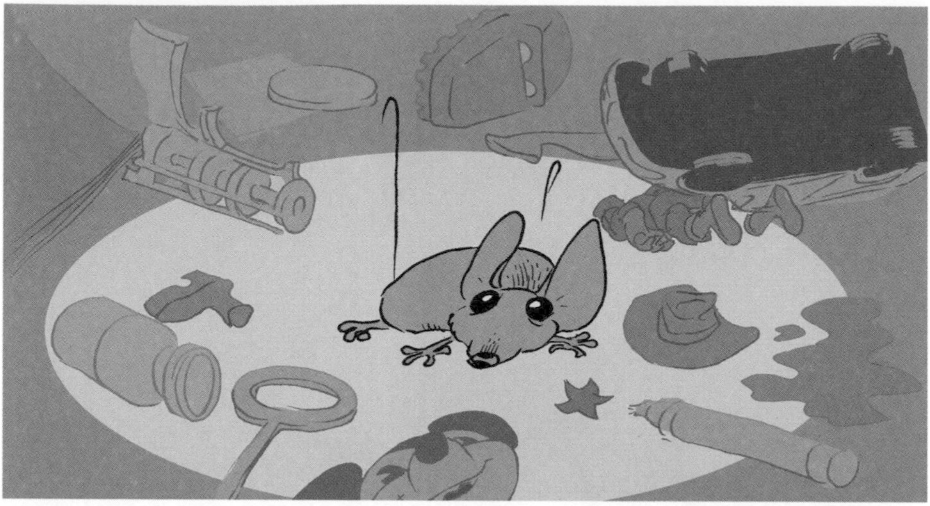

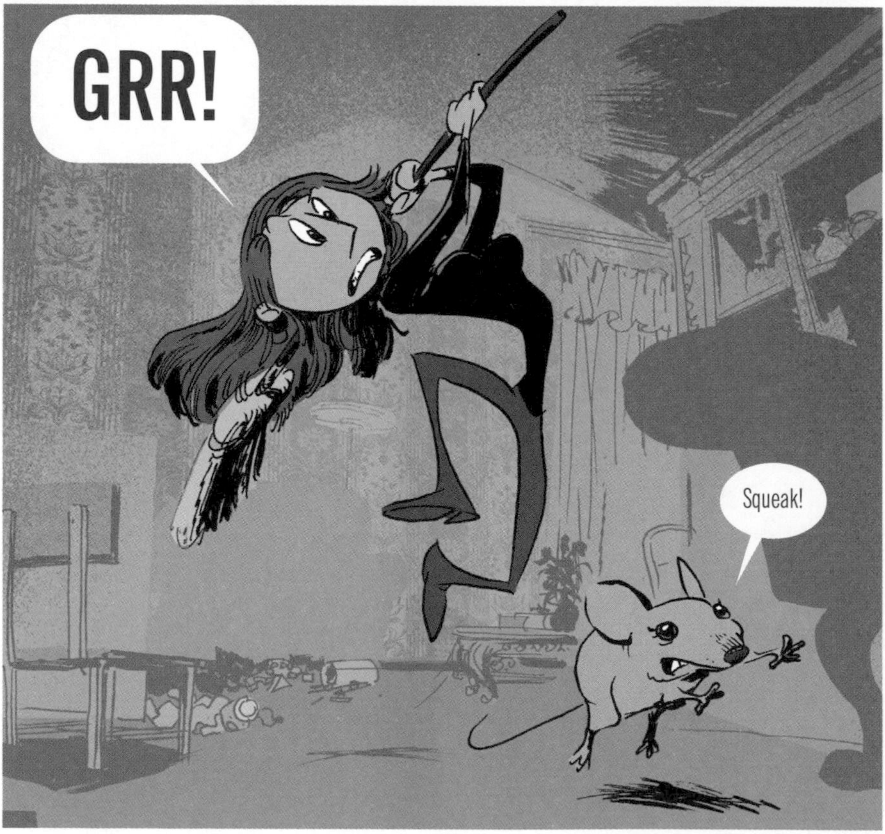
GRR!
Squeak!

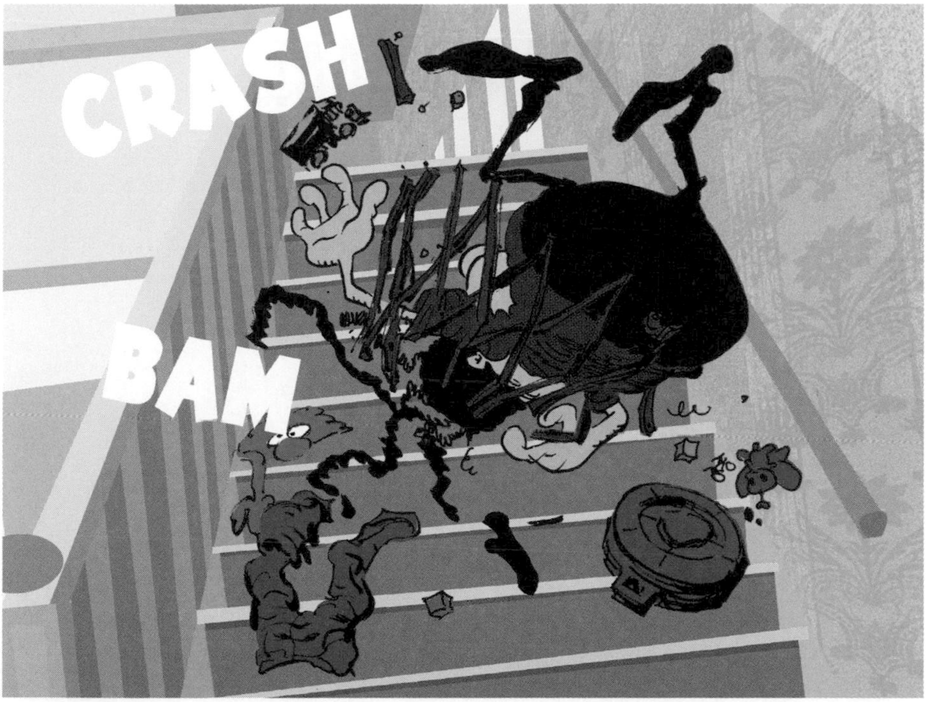
CRASH
BAM

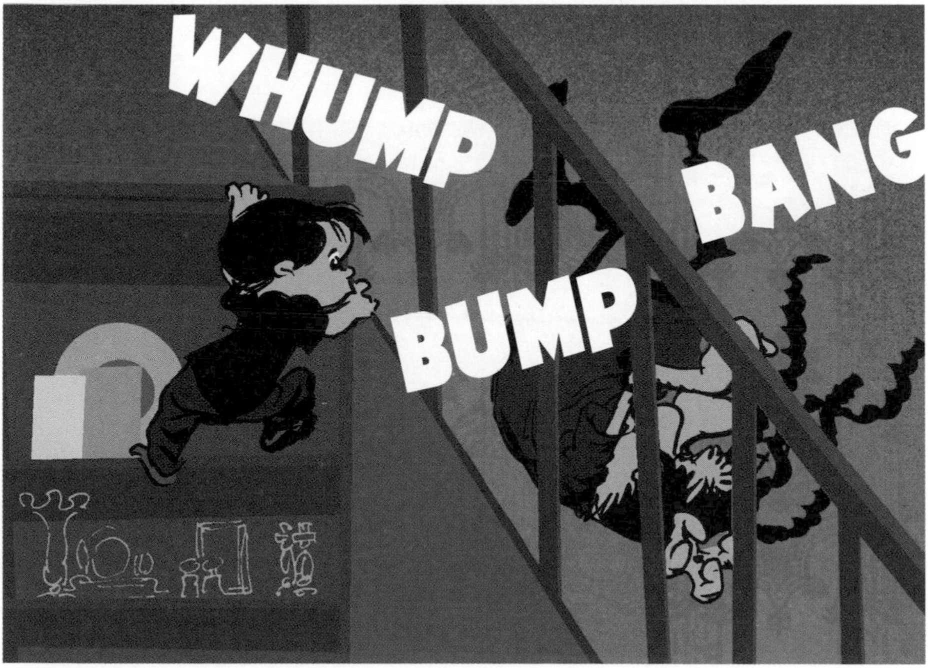
WHUMP
BANG
BUMP

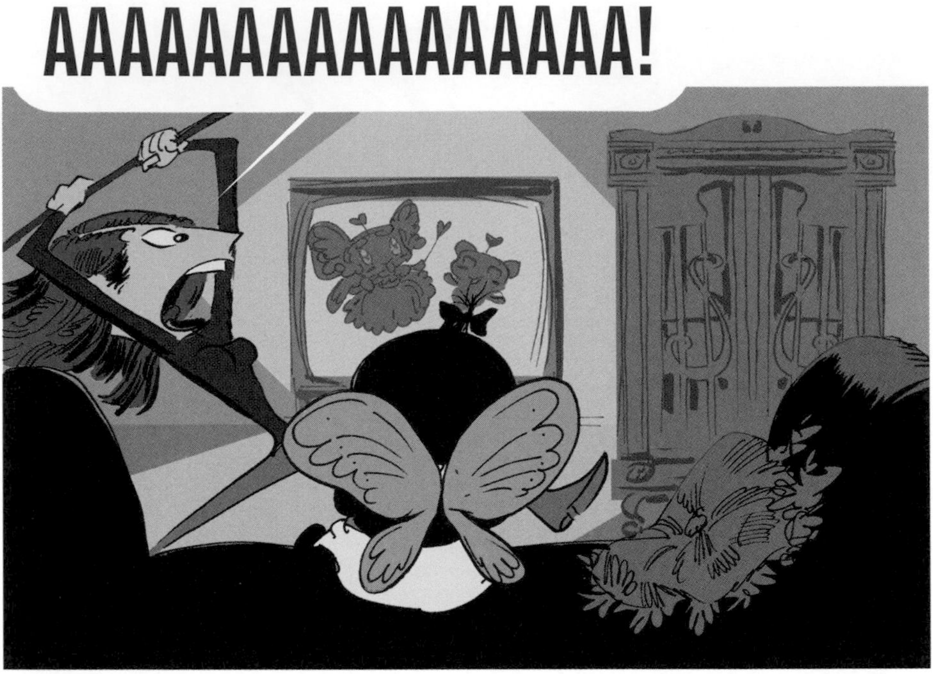
AAAAAAAAAAAAAAAA!

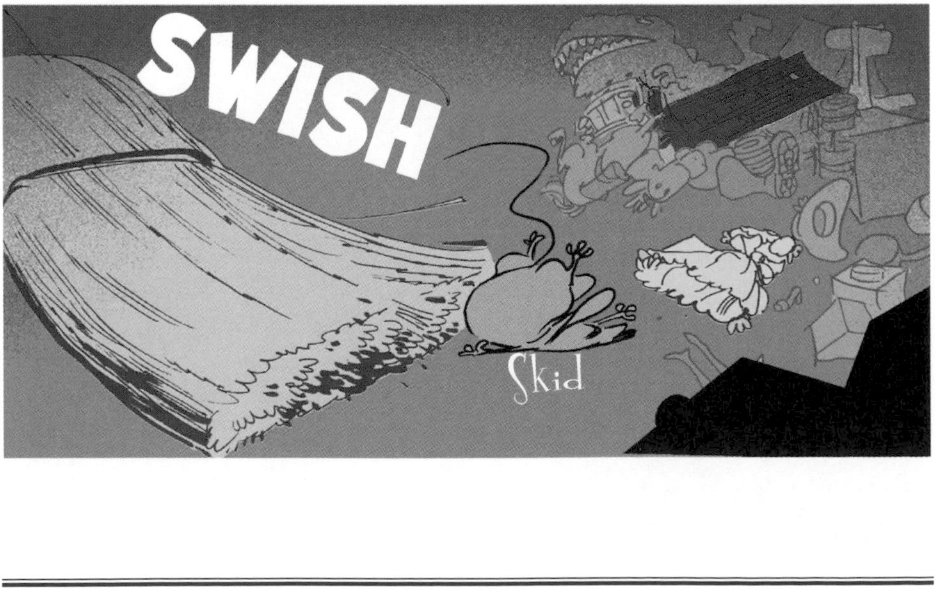
SWISH
Skid

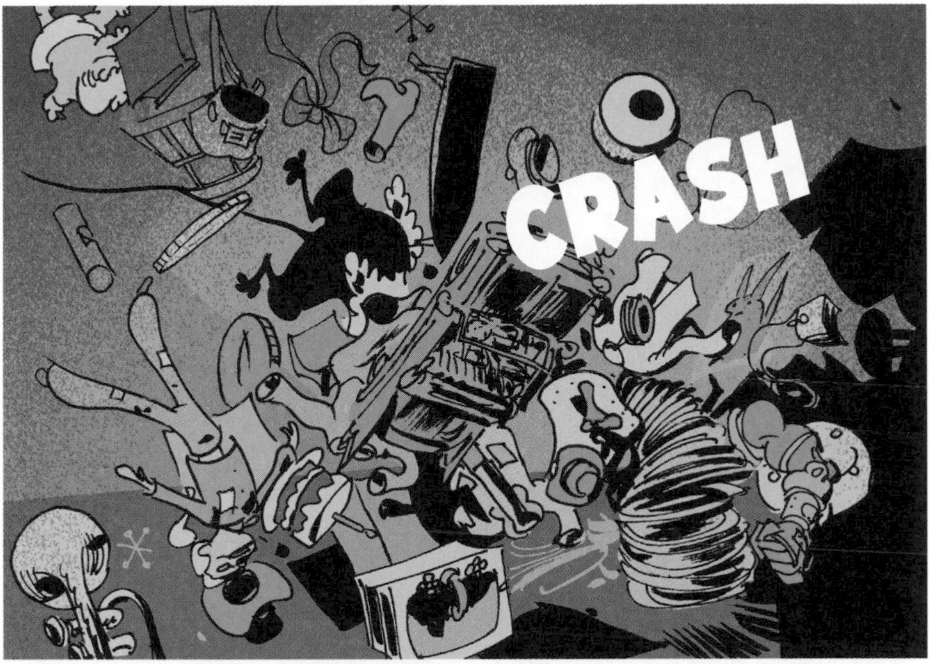
CRASH

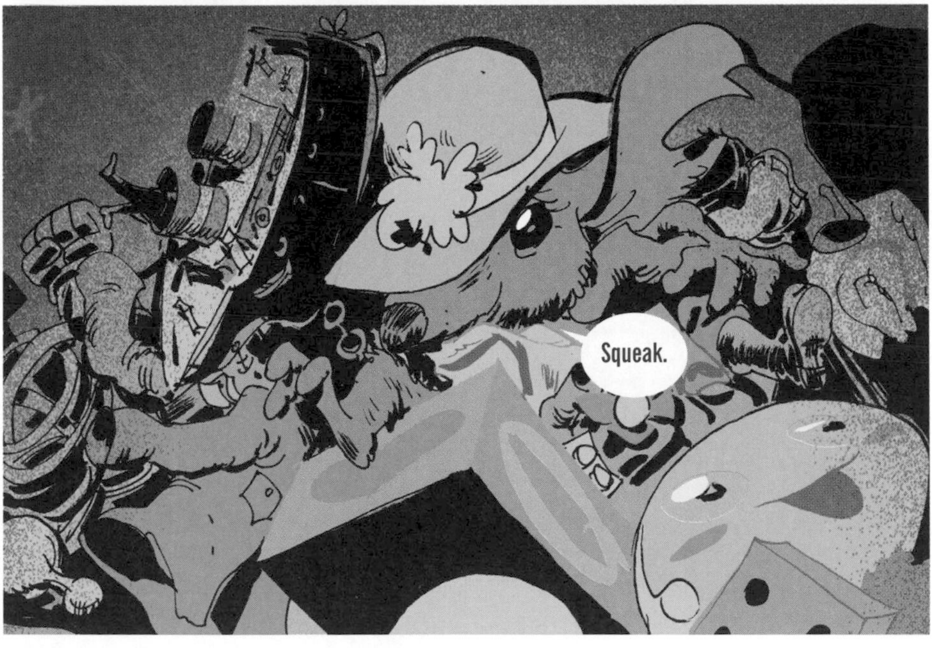
Squeak.

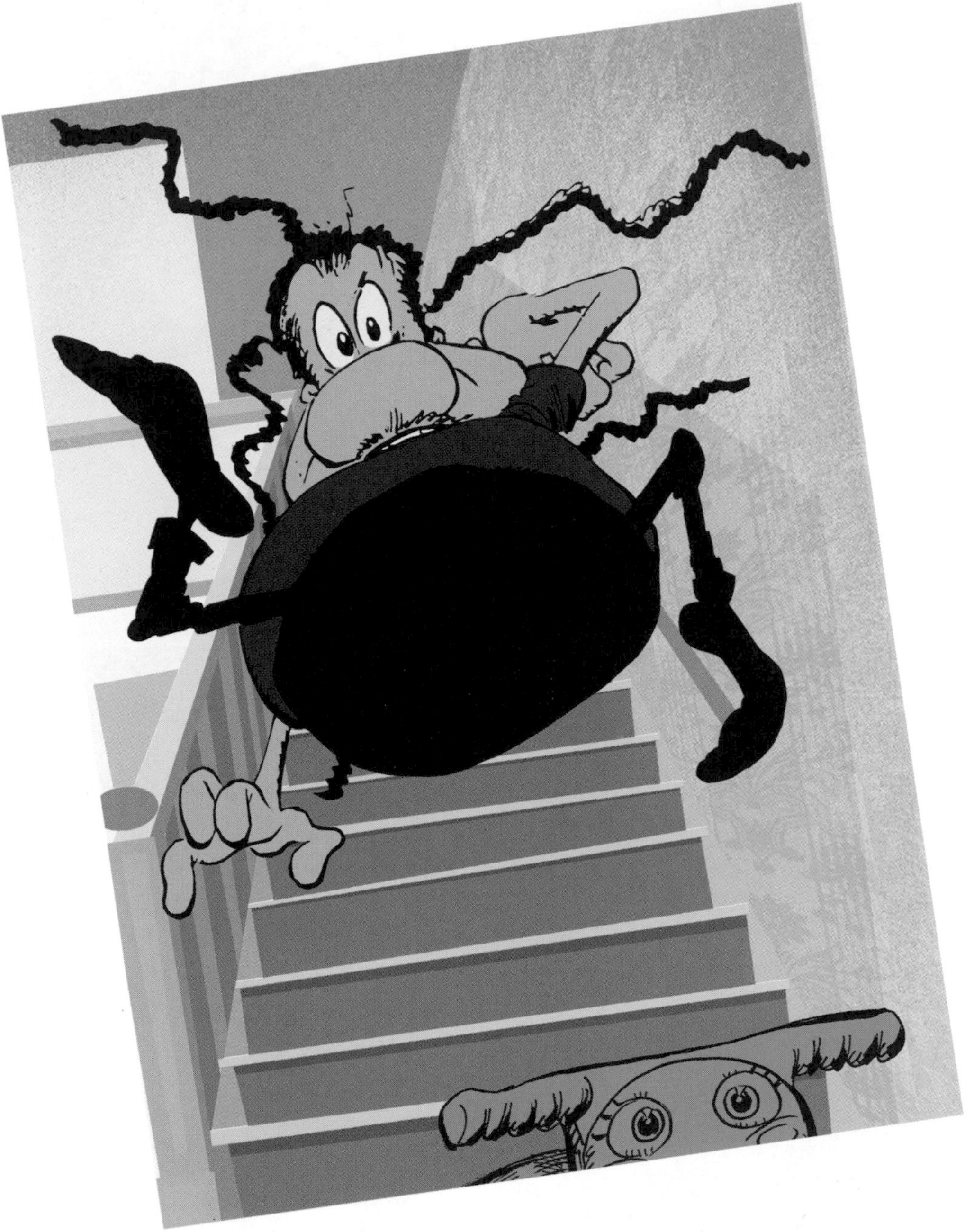

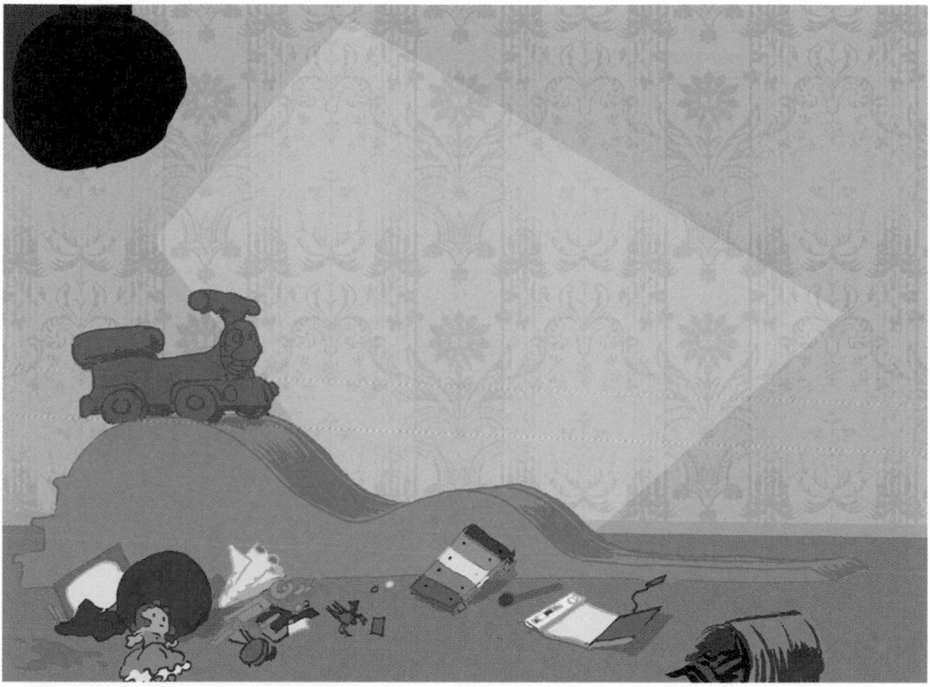

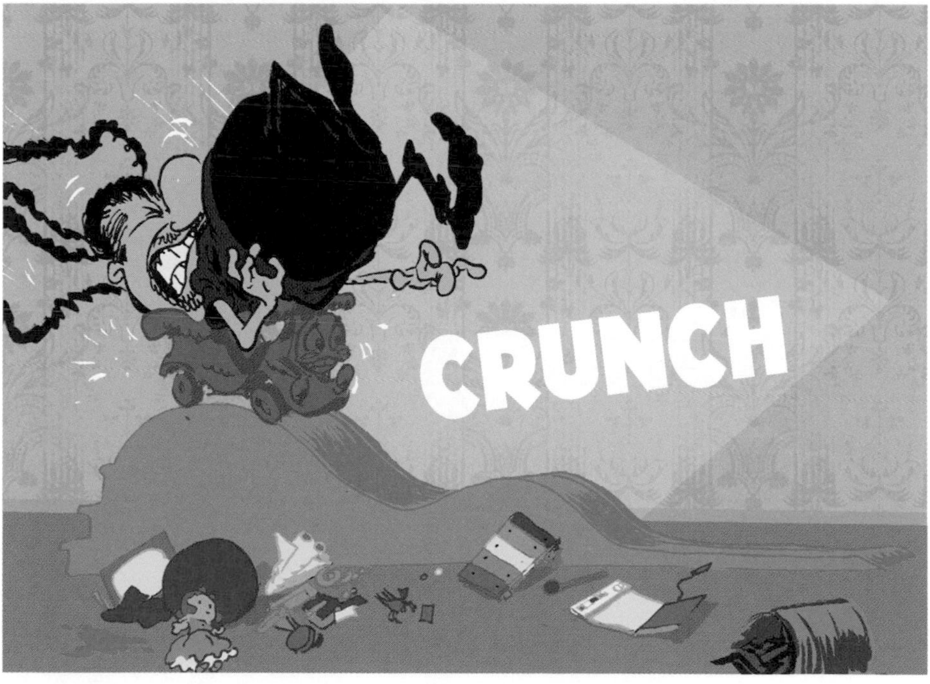
CRUNCH

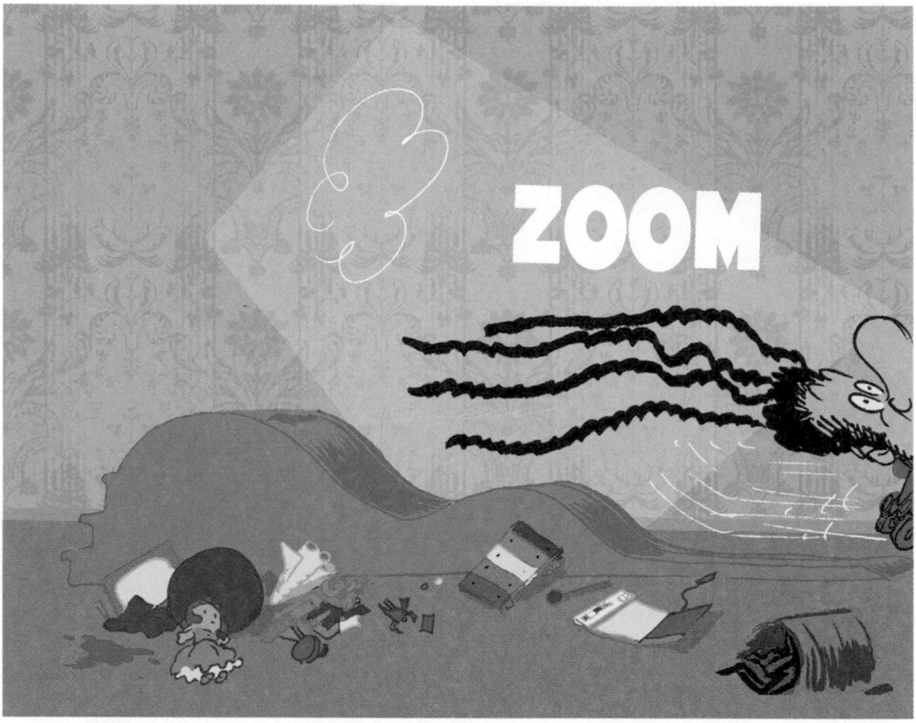
ZOOM

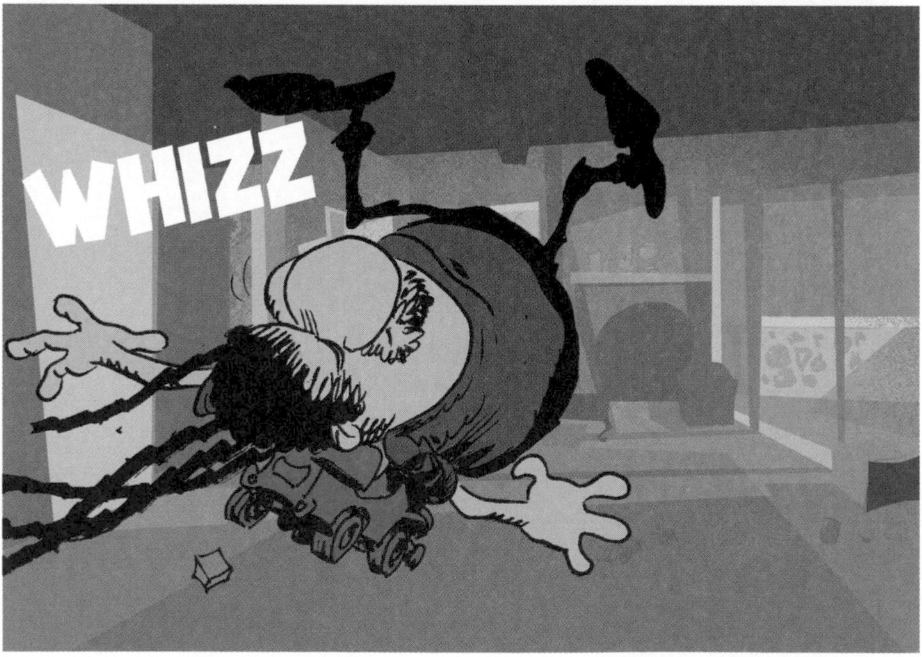
WHIZZ

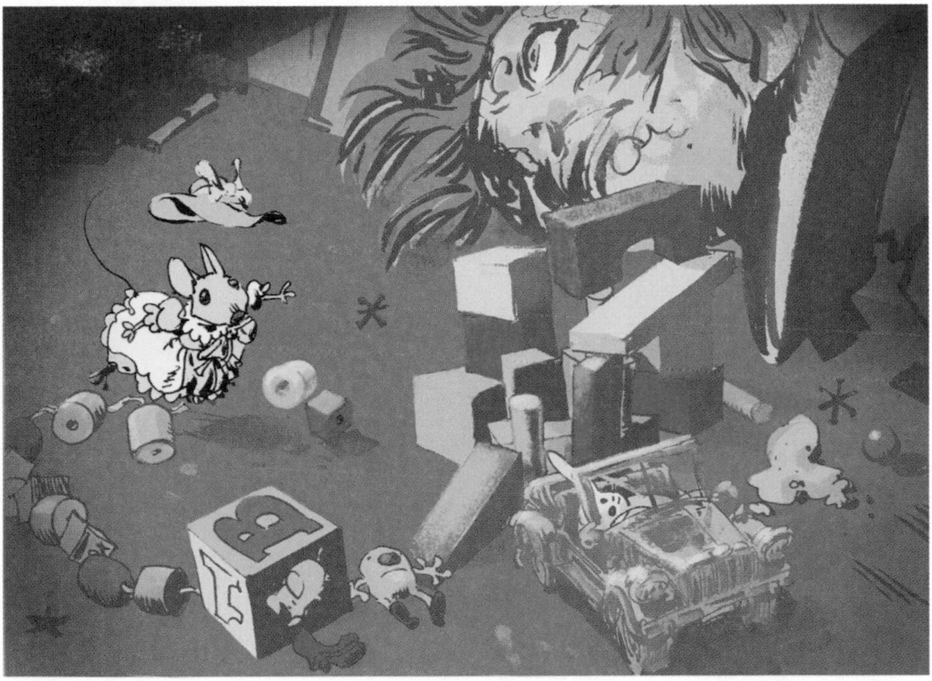

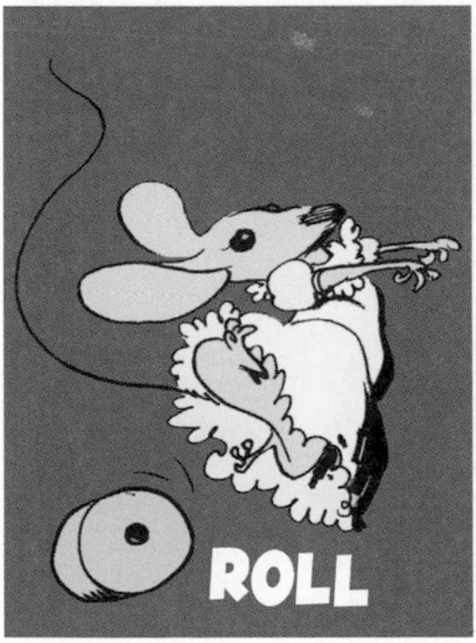
ROLL

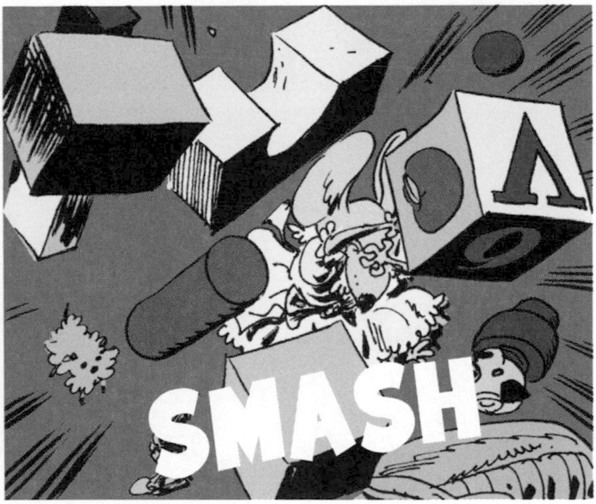
SMASH

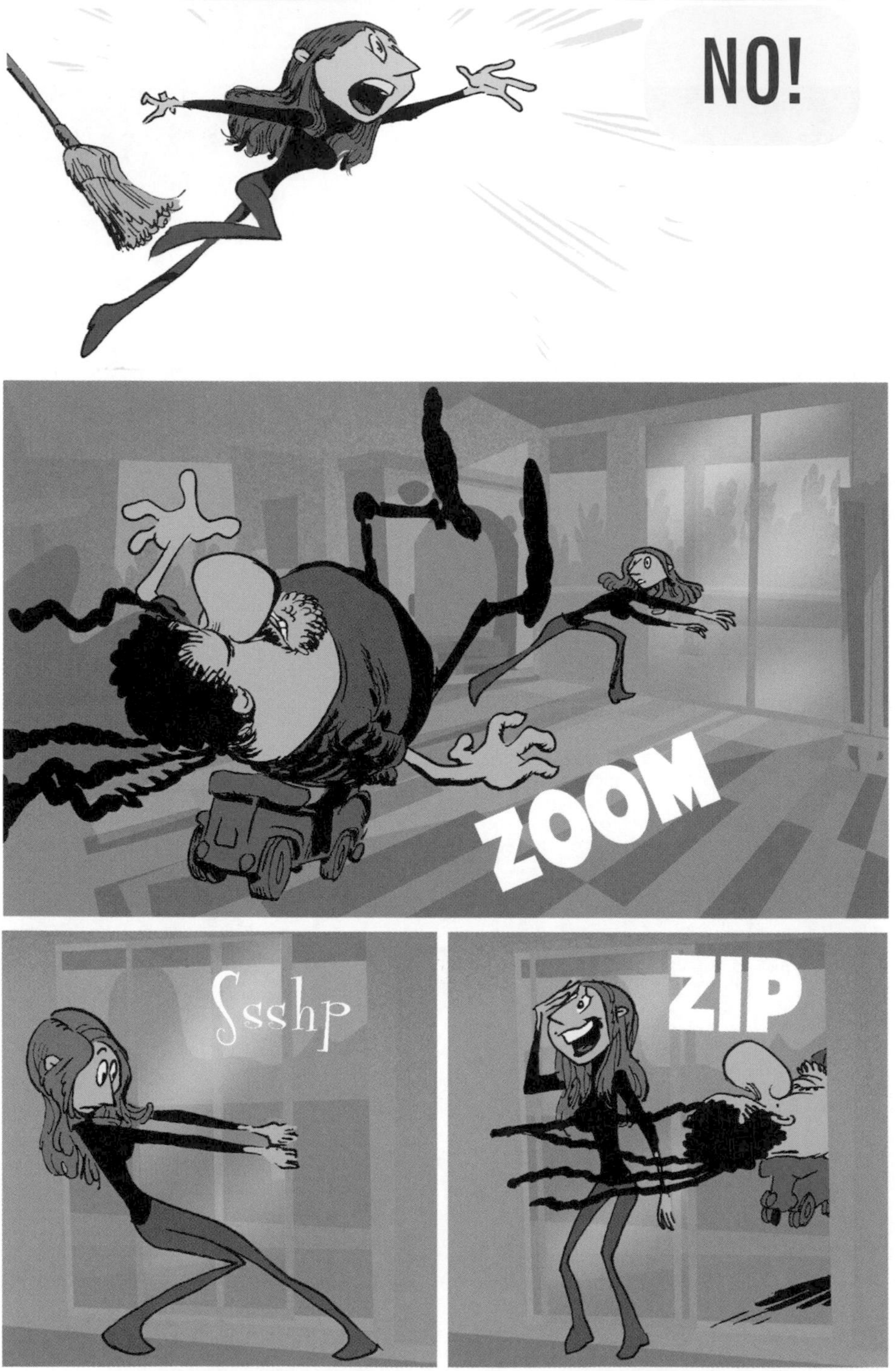
NO!
ZOOM
Ssshp
ZIP

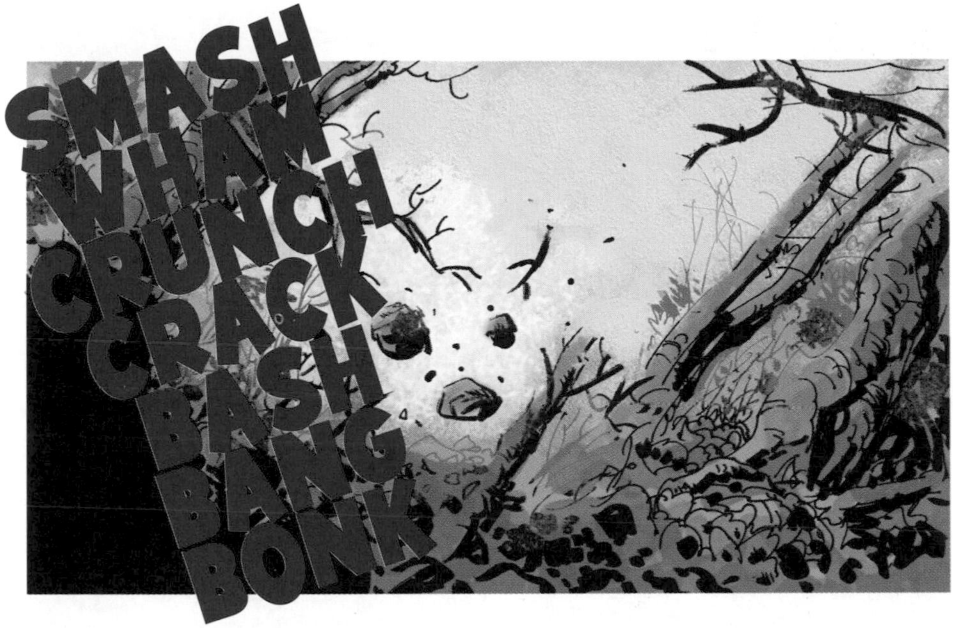
SMASH
WHAM
CRUNCH
CRACK
CRASH
BASH
BANG
BONK

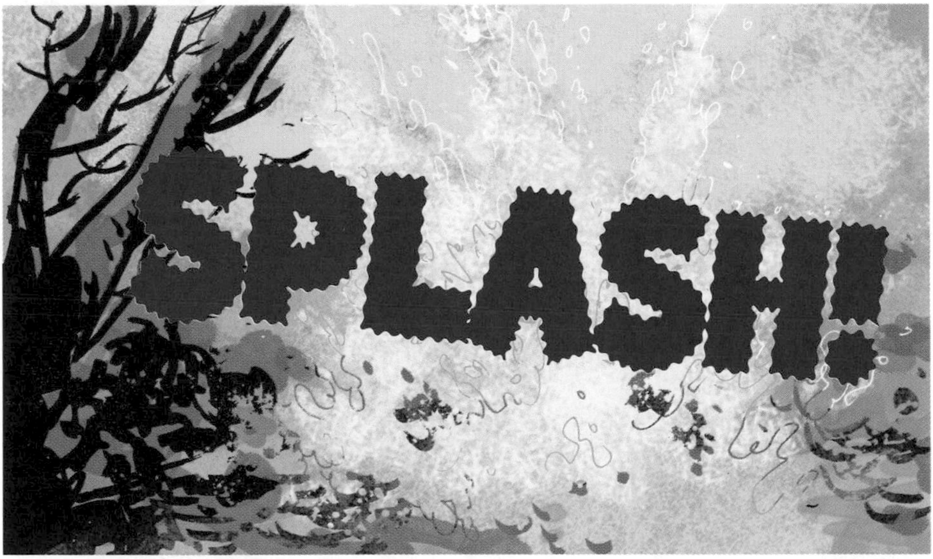
SPLASH!

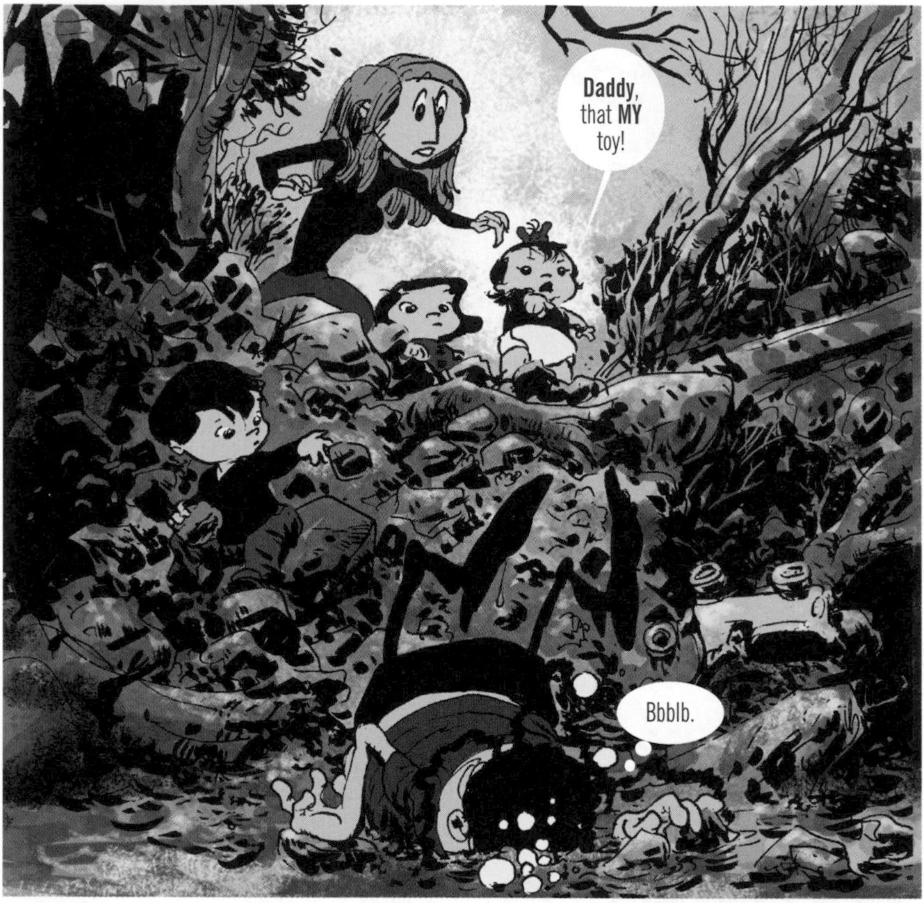
Daddy, that MY toy!
Bbblb.

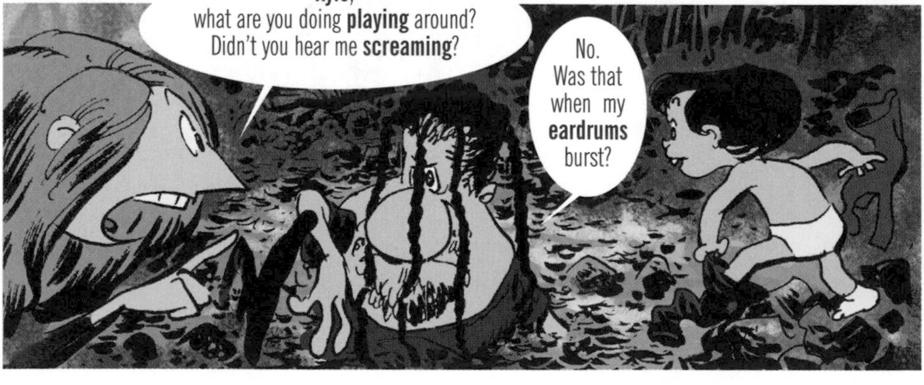
Kyle, what are you doing playing around? Didn't you hear me screaming?
No. Was that when my eardrums burst?

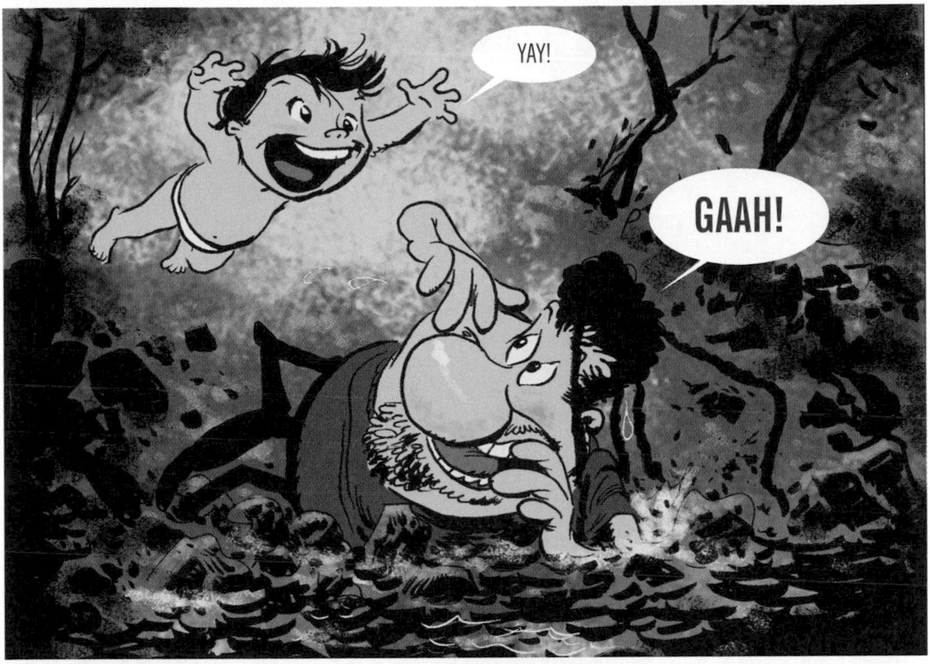
YAY!
GAAH!

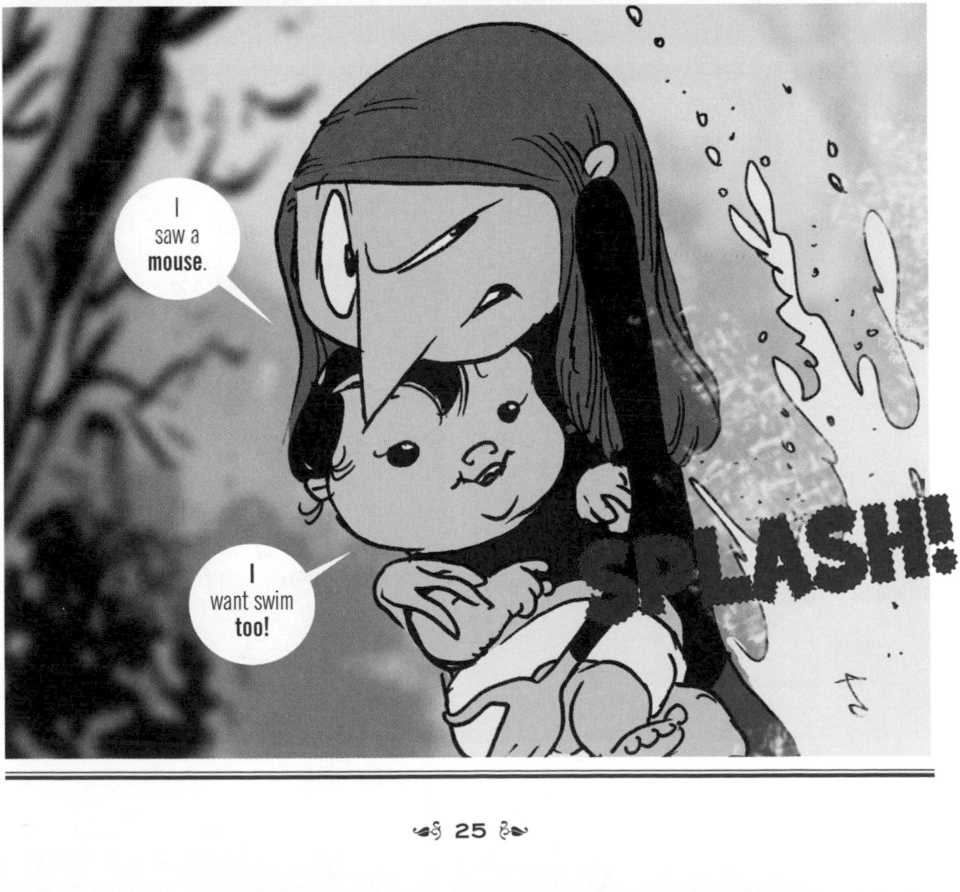
I saw a **mouse**.
I want swim **too!**
SPLASH!

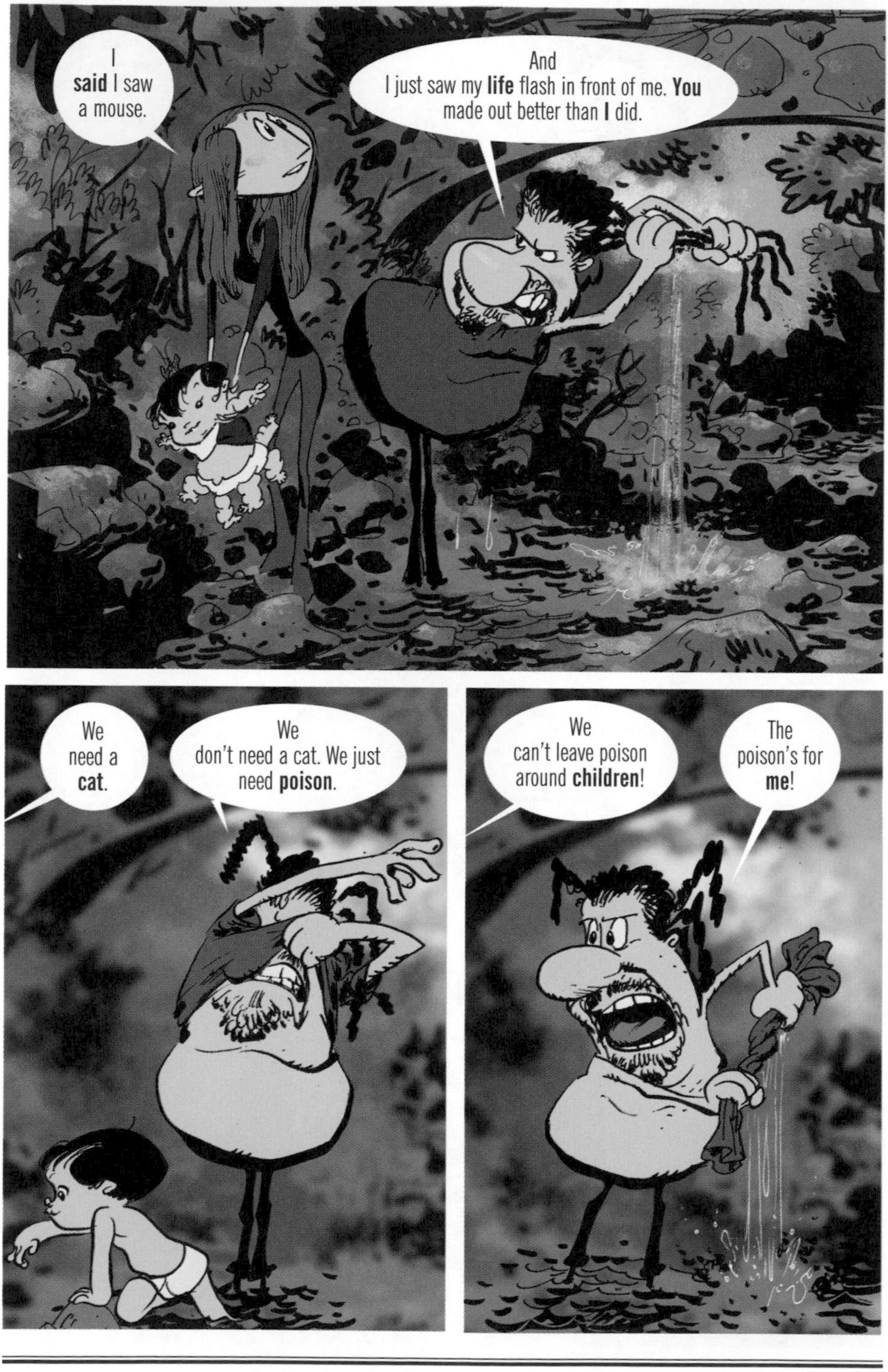
I **said** I saw a mouse.
And I just saw my **life** flash in front of me. **You** made out better than **I** did.
We need a **cat**.
We don't need a cat. We just need **poison**.
We can't leave poison around **children**!
The poison's for **me**!

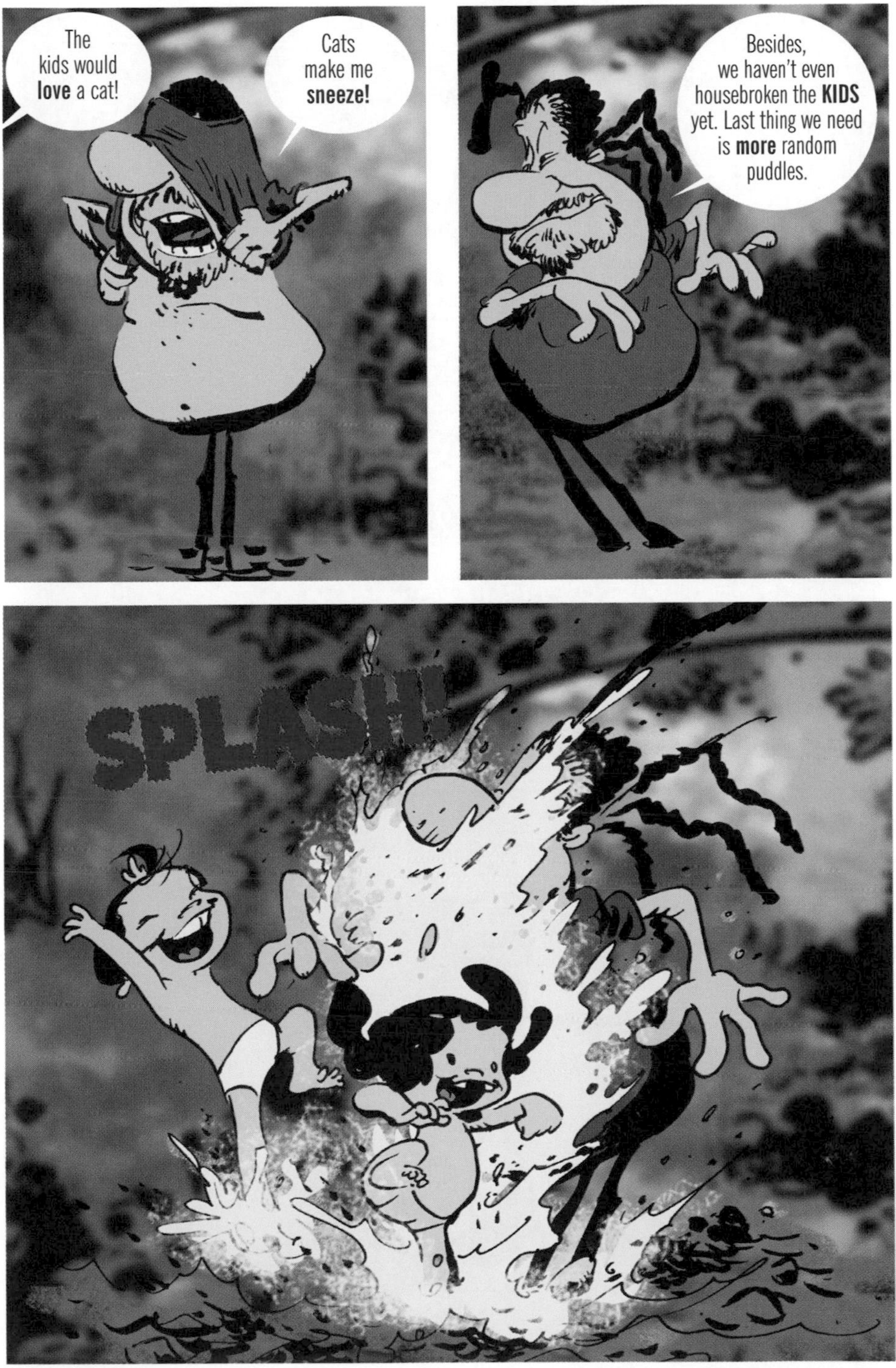
The kids would love a cat!
Cats make me sneeze!
Besides, we haven't even housebroken the KIDS yet. Last thing we need is more random puddles.
SPLASH!

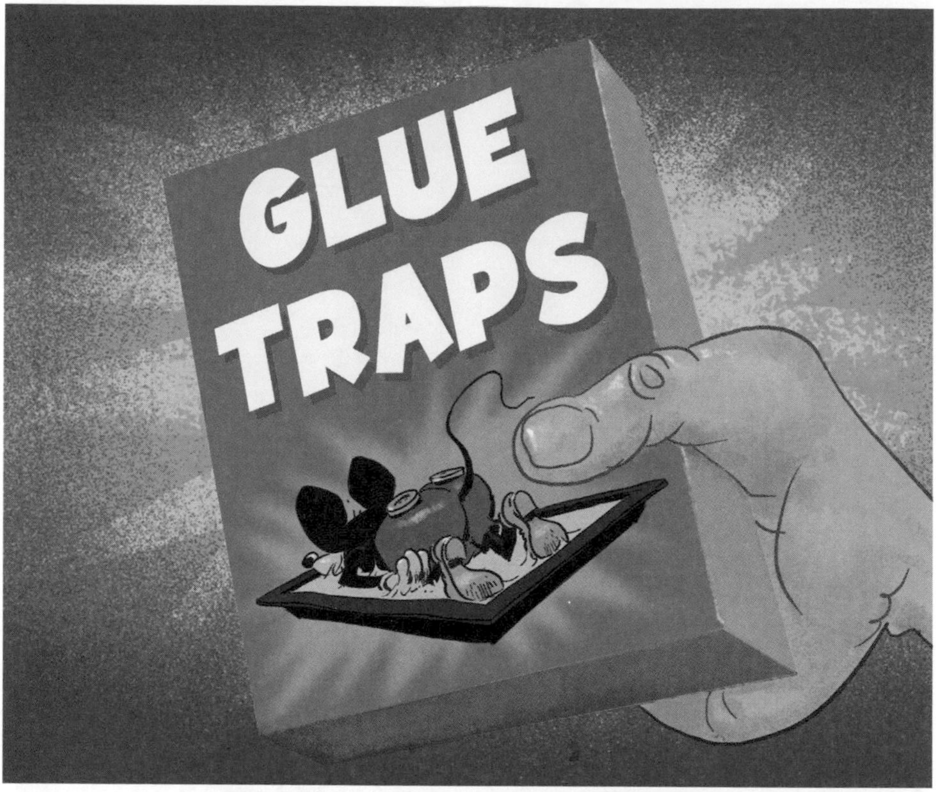
GLUE
TRAPS

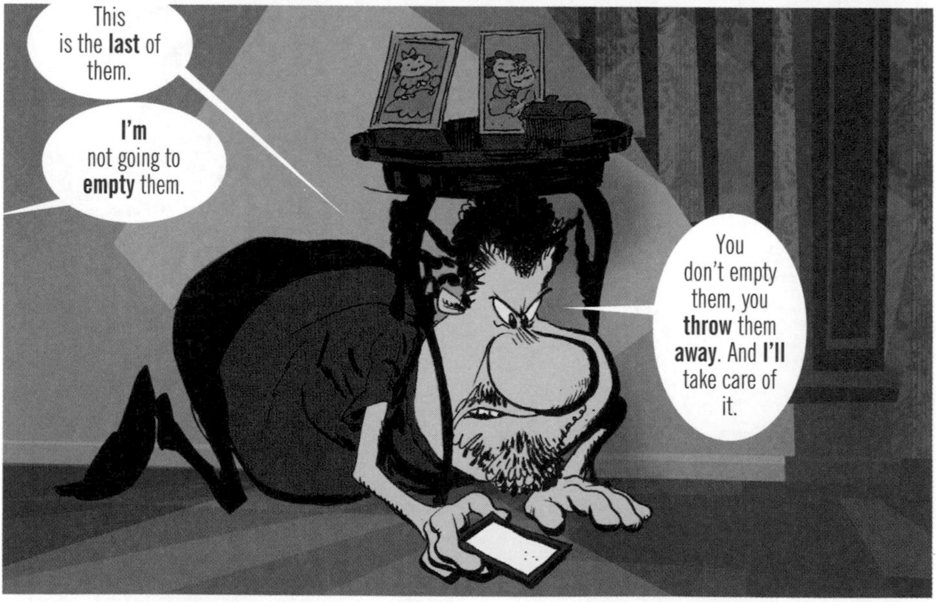
This is the **last** of them.
I'm not going to **empty** them.
You don't empty them, you **throw** them **away**. And **I'll** take care of it.

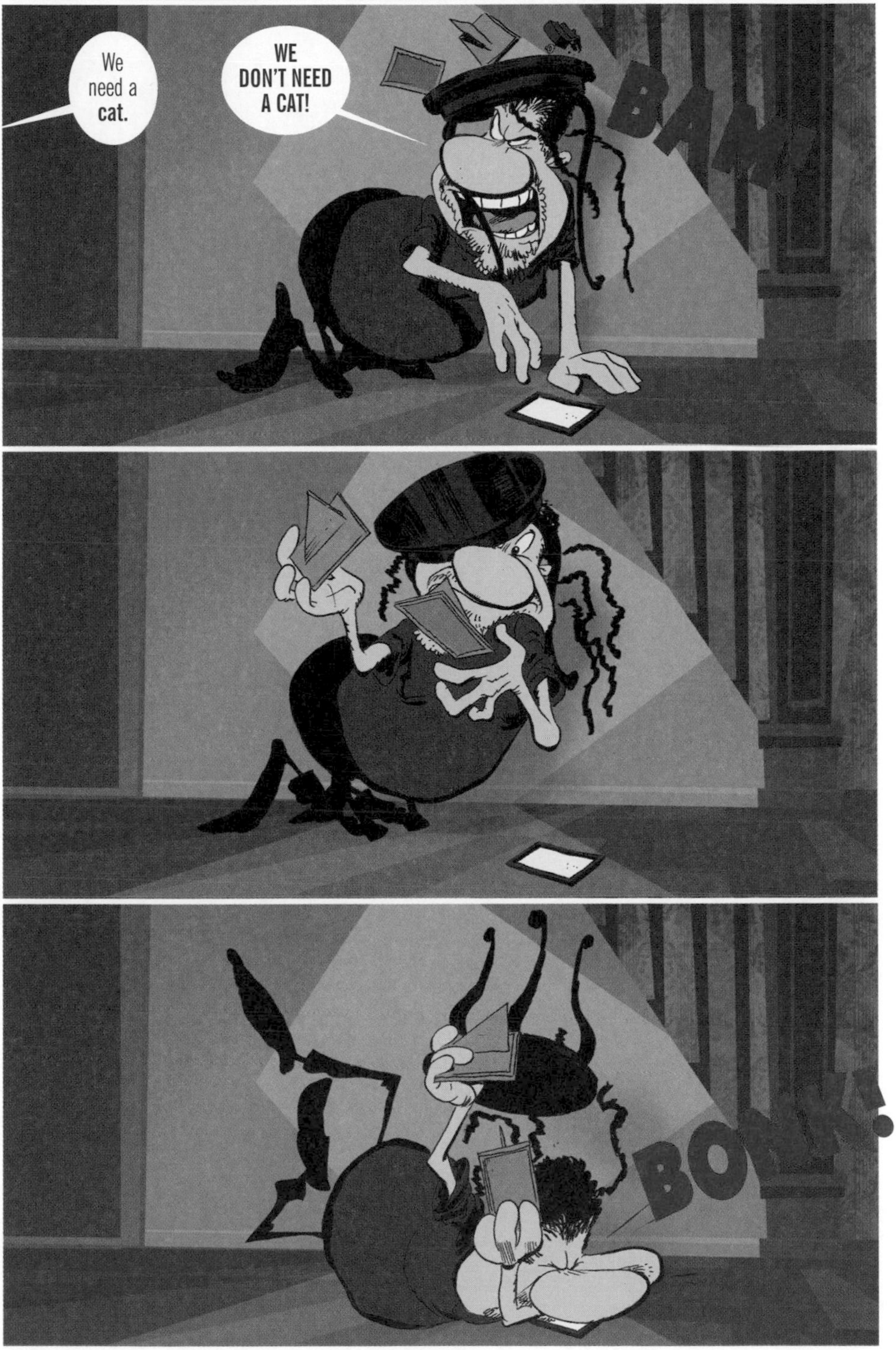
We need a cat.
WE DON'T NEED A CAT!
BAM
BONK!

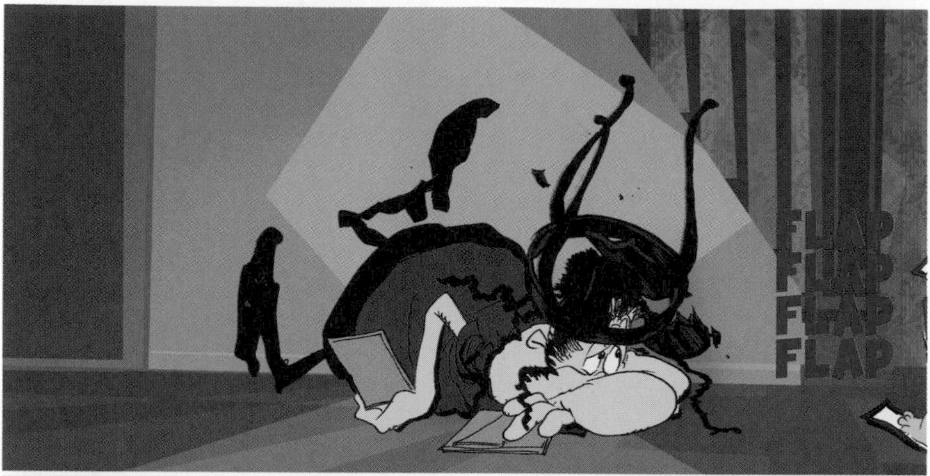
FLAP
FLAP
FLAP
FLAP

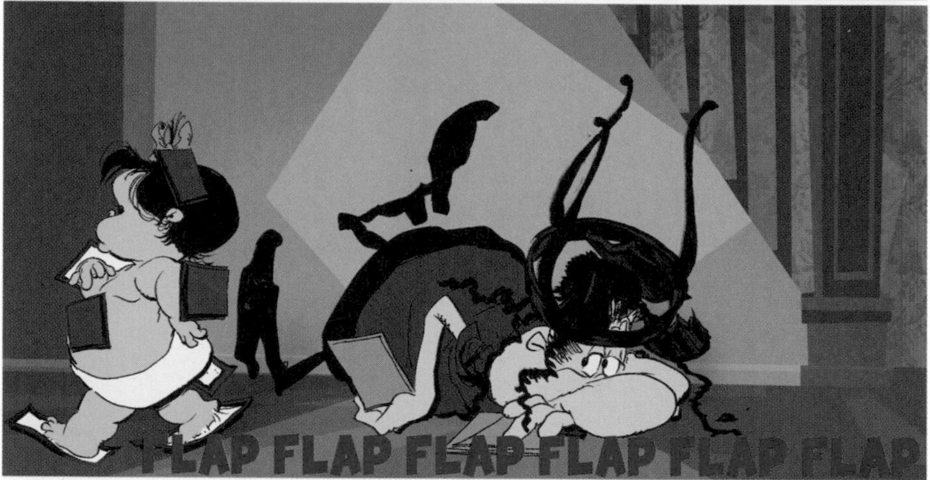
FLAP FLAP FLAP FLAP FLAP FLAP

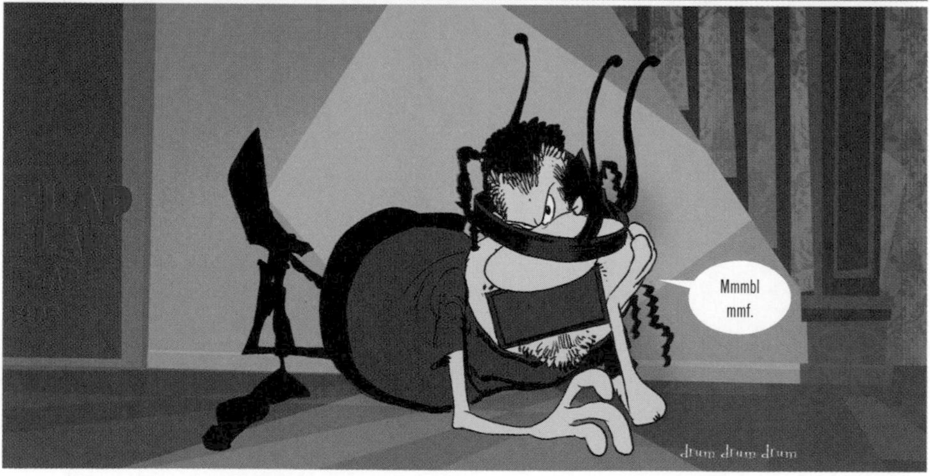
FLAP
Mmmbl mmf.
drum drum drum

I want sleep with **Mommy.**
Jackie, you're a **big** girl now, and it's time to sleep in your **new** big girl **bed**.
Good night, everyone.
Precious Pixies

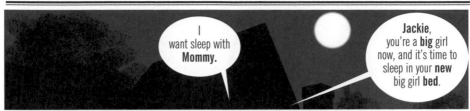

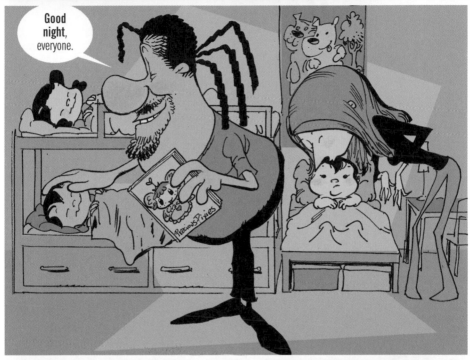

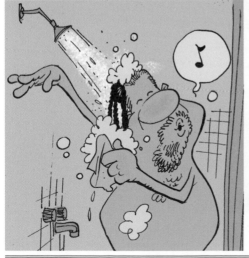

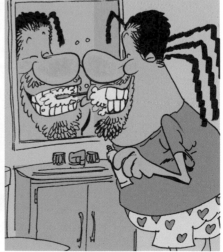

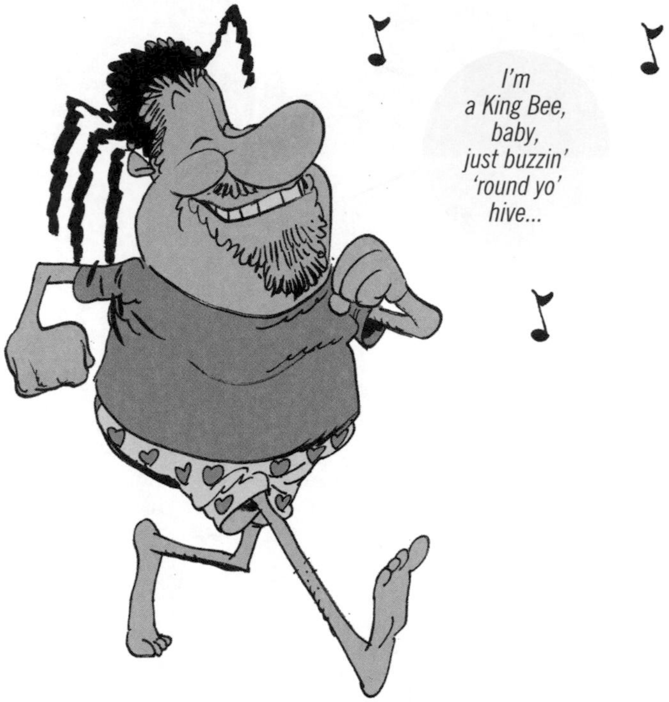
I'm a King Bee, baby, just buzzin' 'round yo' hive...

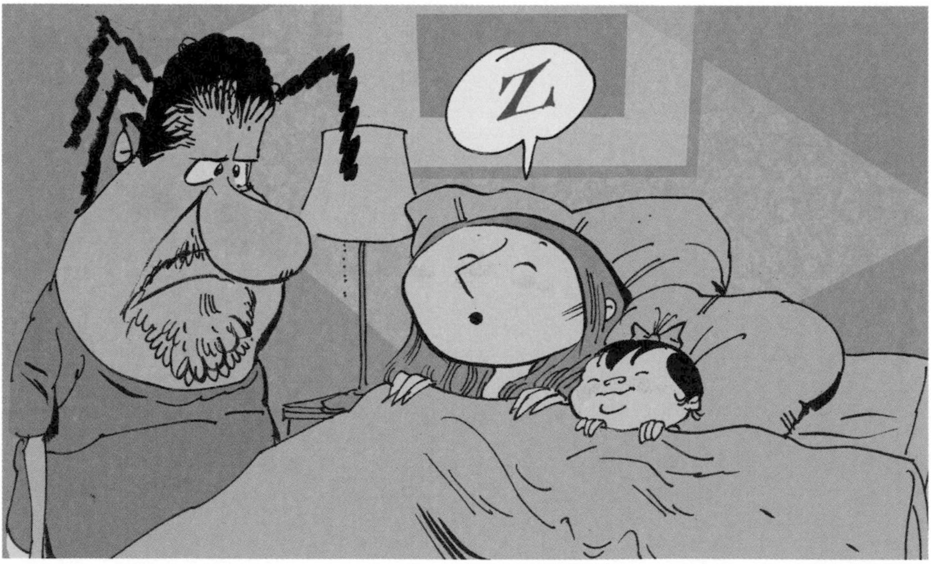
Z

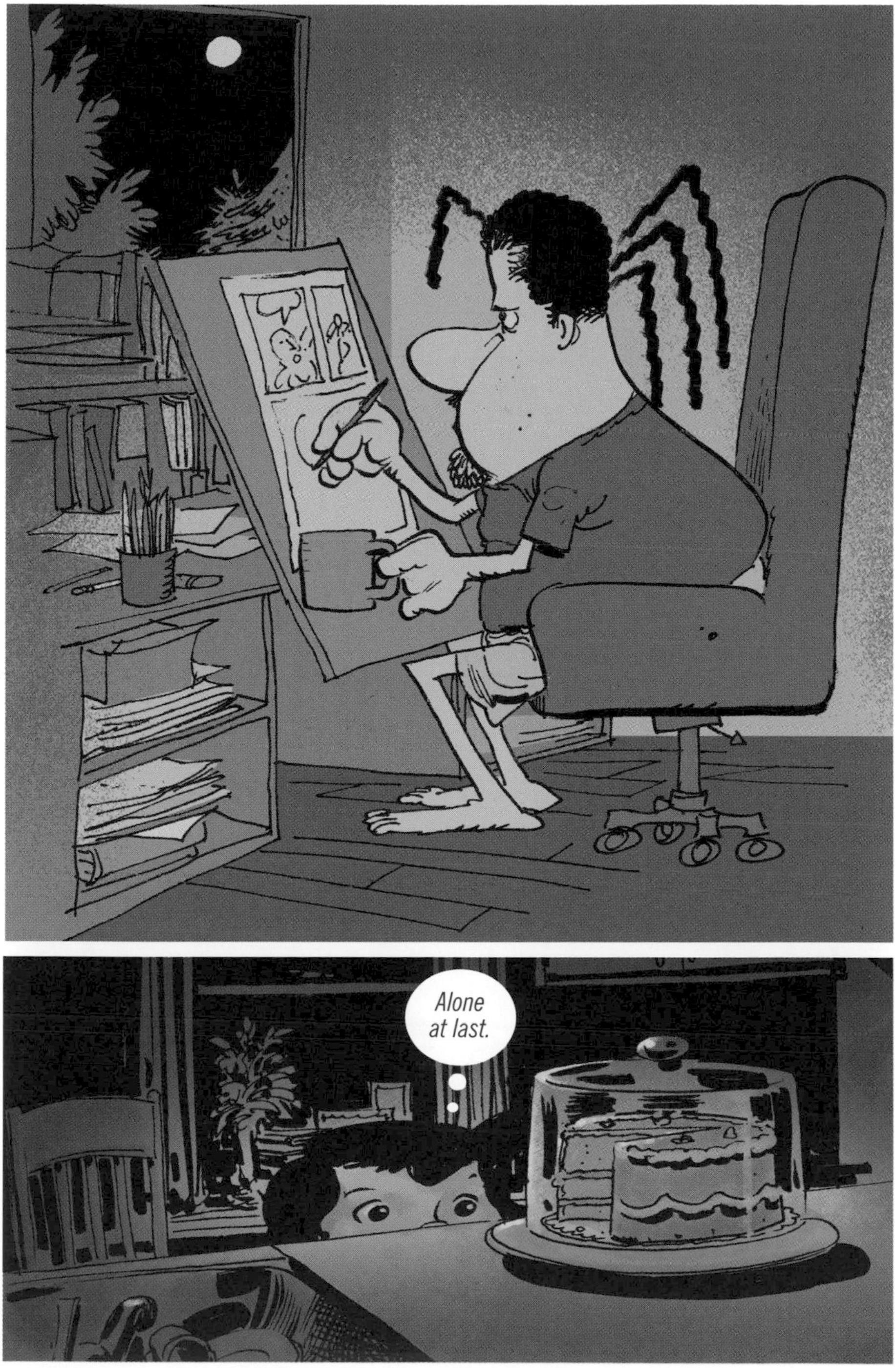
Alone
at last.

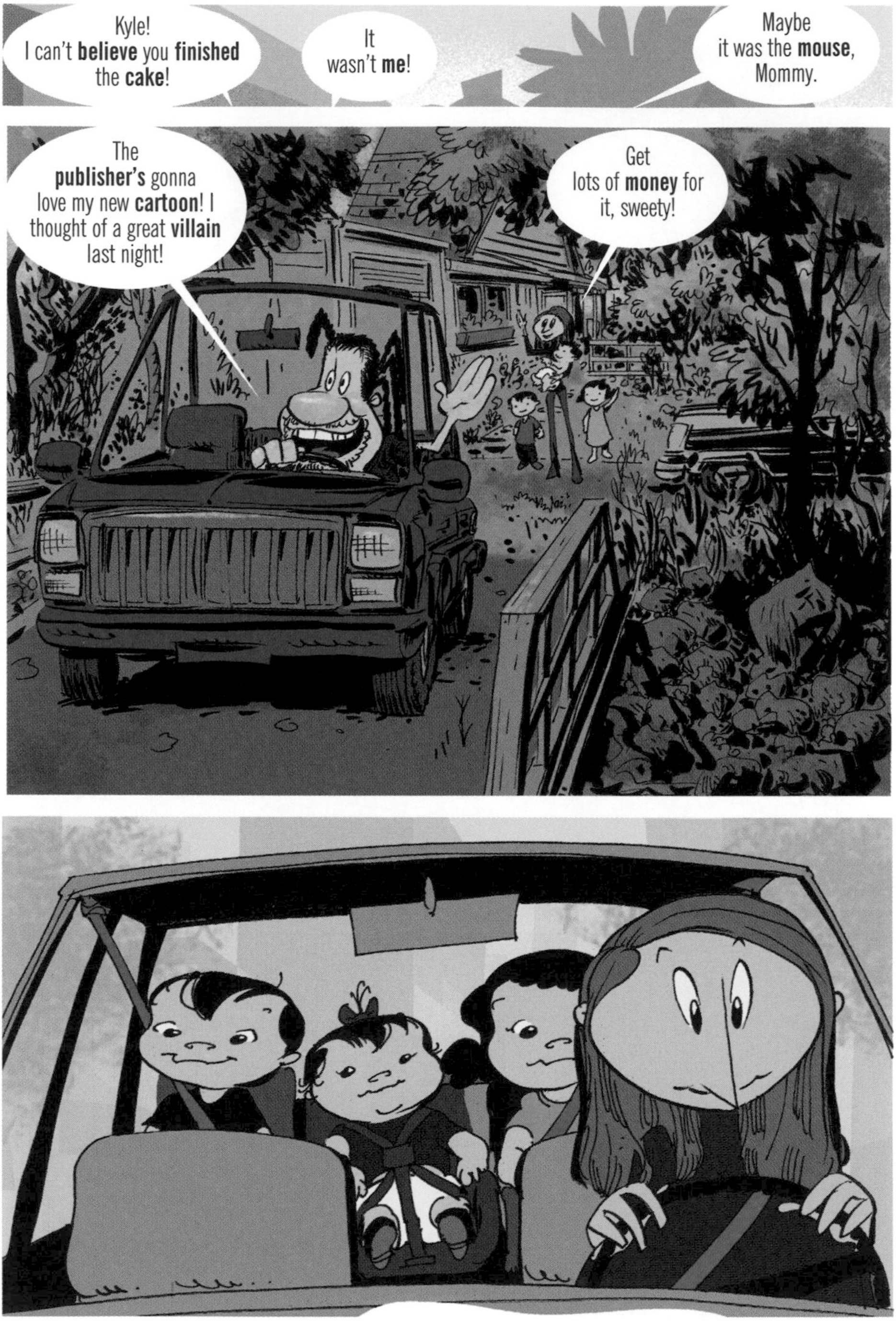
Kyle!
I can't **believe** you **finished** the **cake**!
It wasn't **me**!
Maybe it was the **mouse**, Mommy.
The **publisher's** gonna love my new **cartoon**! I thought of a great **villain** last night!
Get lots of **money** for it, sweety!

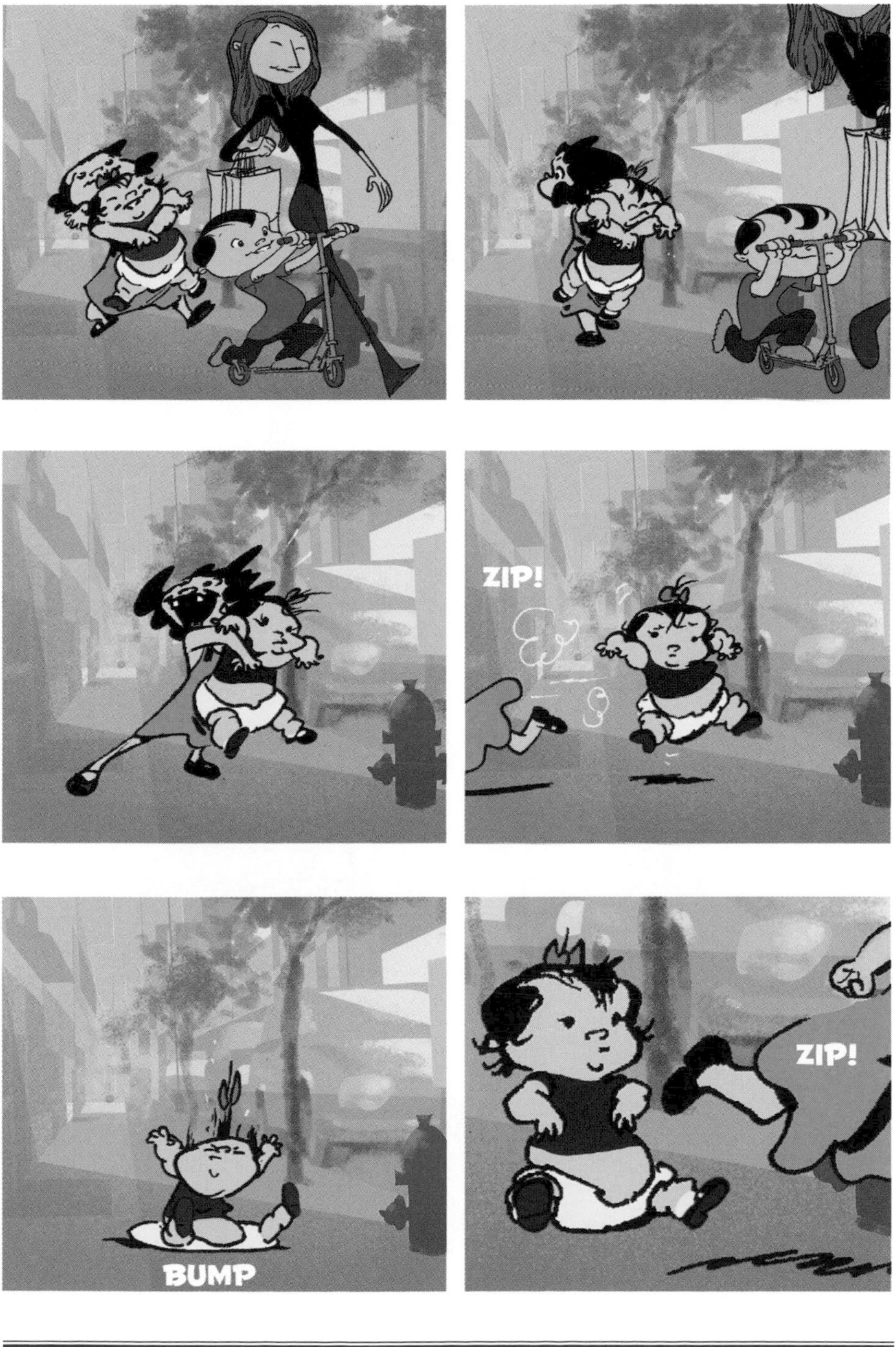
ZIP!
BUMP
ZIP!

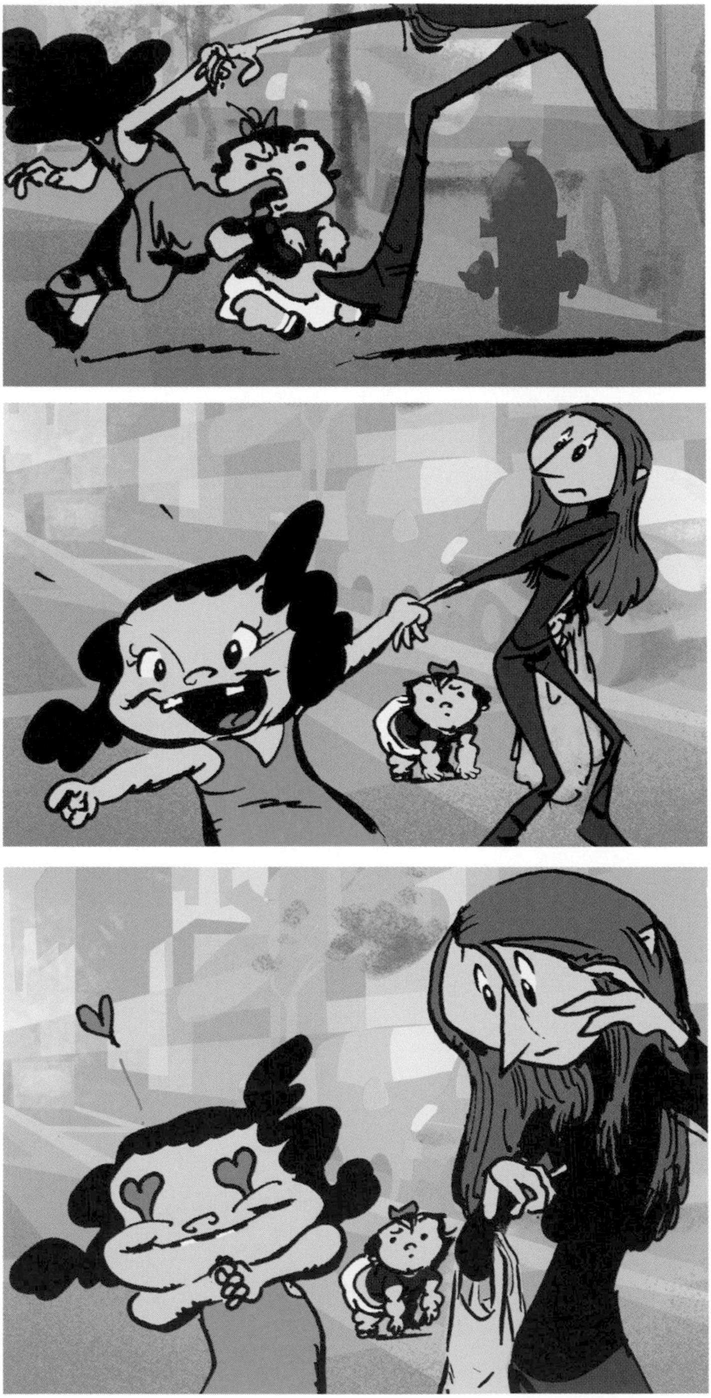

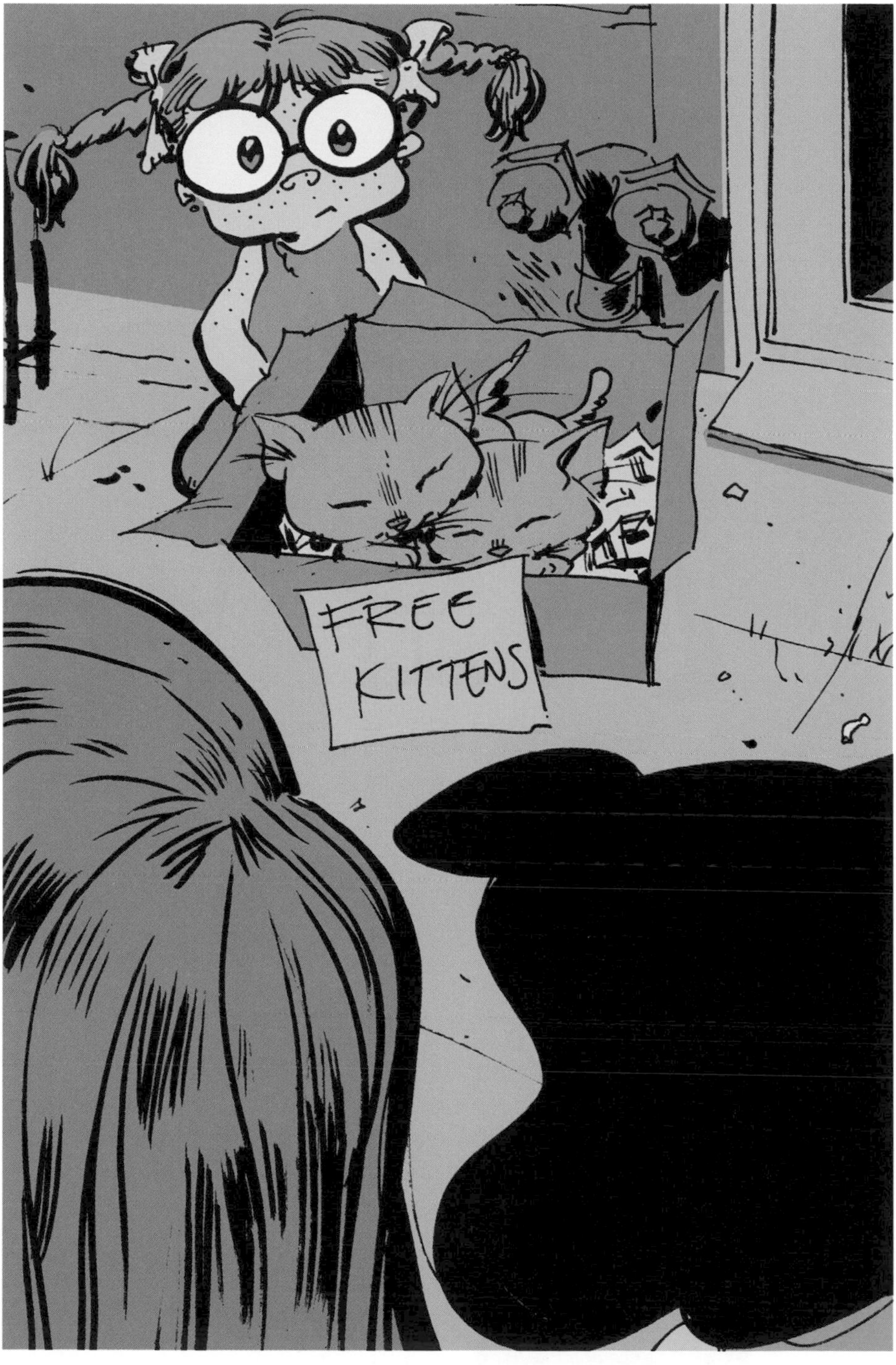
FREE
KITTENS

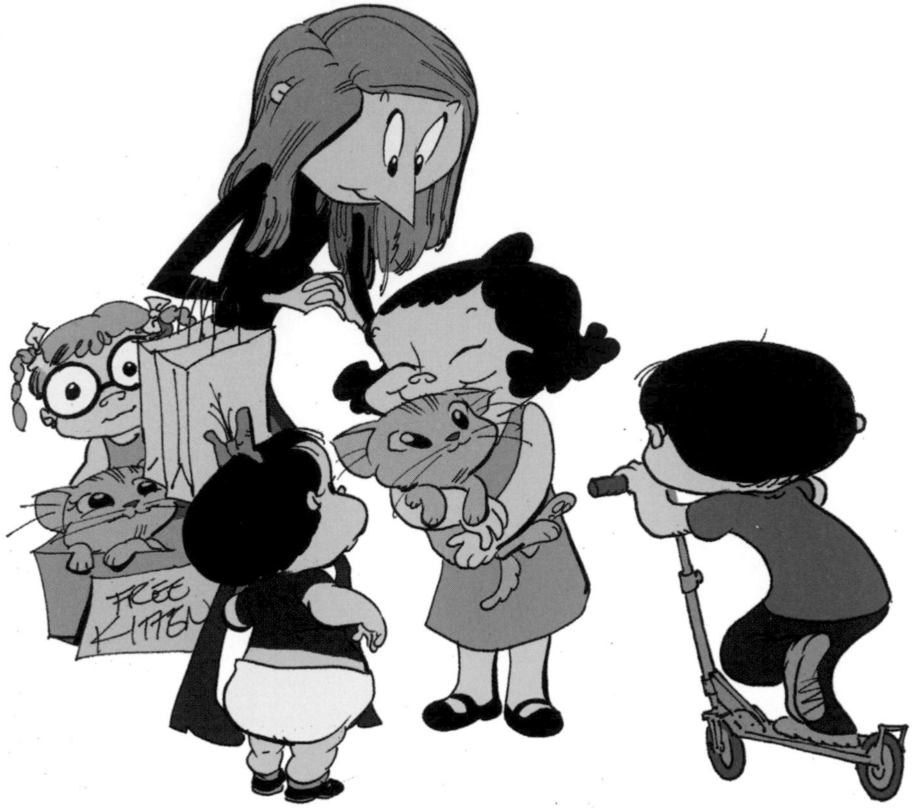
FREE KITTENS

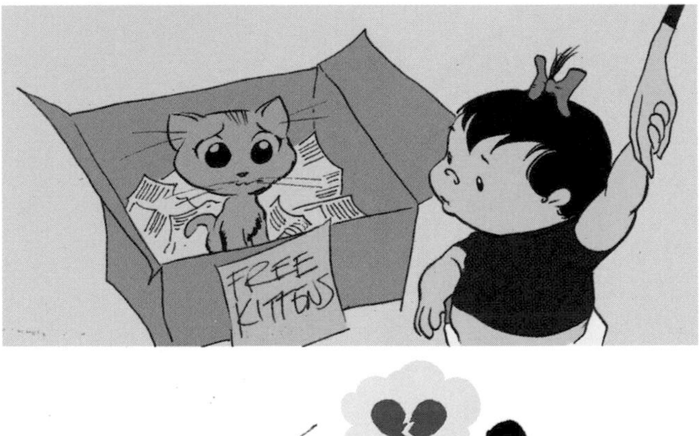
FREE KITTENS

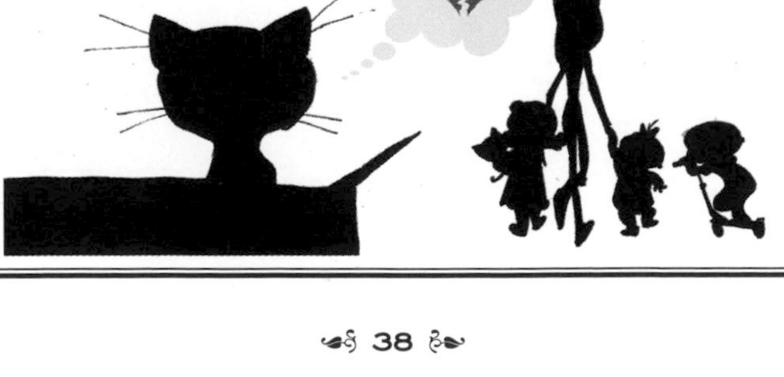

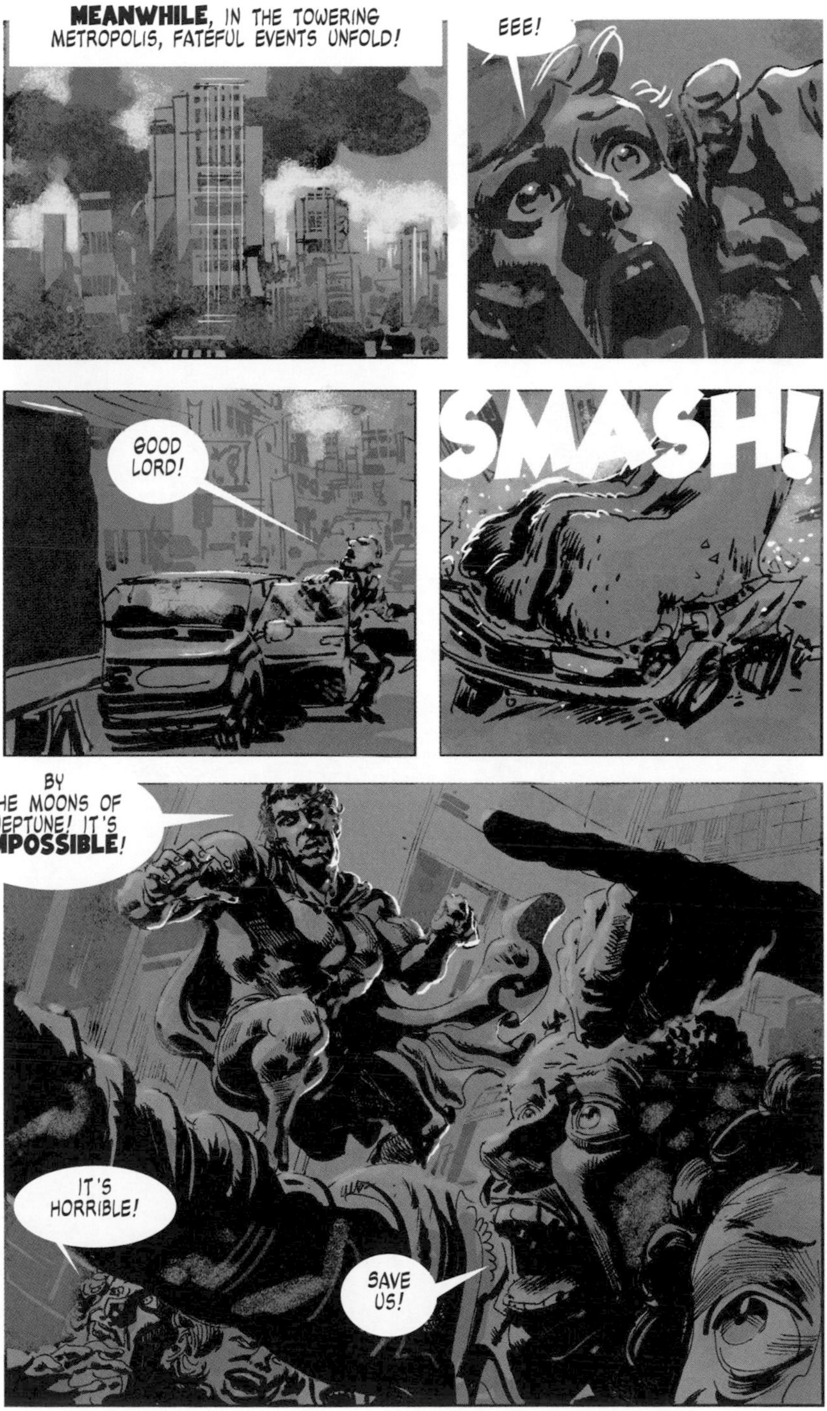
MEANWHILE, IN THE TOWERING METROPOLIS, FATEFUL EVENTS UNFOLD!
EEE!
GOOD LORD!
SMASH!
BY THE MOONS OF NEPTUNE! IT'S IMPOSSIBLE!
IT'S HORRIBLE!
SAVE US!

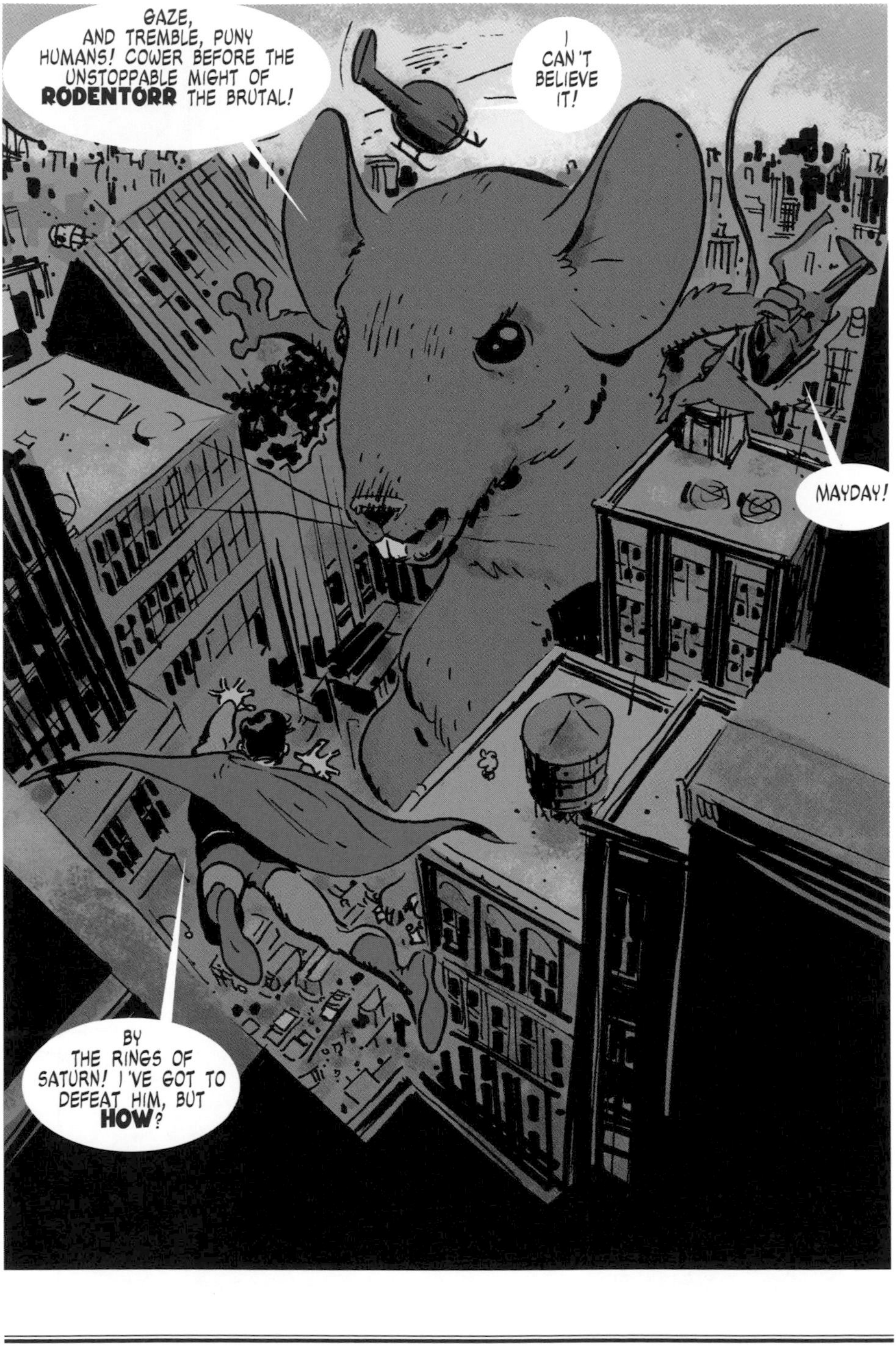
GAZE, AND TREMBLE, PUNY HUMANS! COWER BEFORE THE UNSTOPPABLE MIGHT OF **RODENTORR** THE BRUTAL!
I CAN'T BELIEVE IT!
MAYDAY!
BY THE RINGS OF SATURN! I'VE GOT TO DEFEAT HIM, BUT **HOW**?

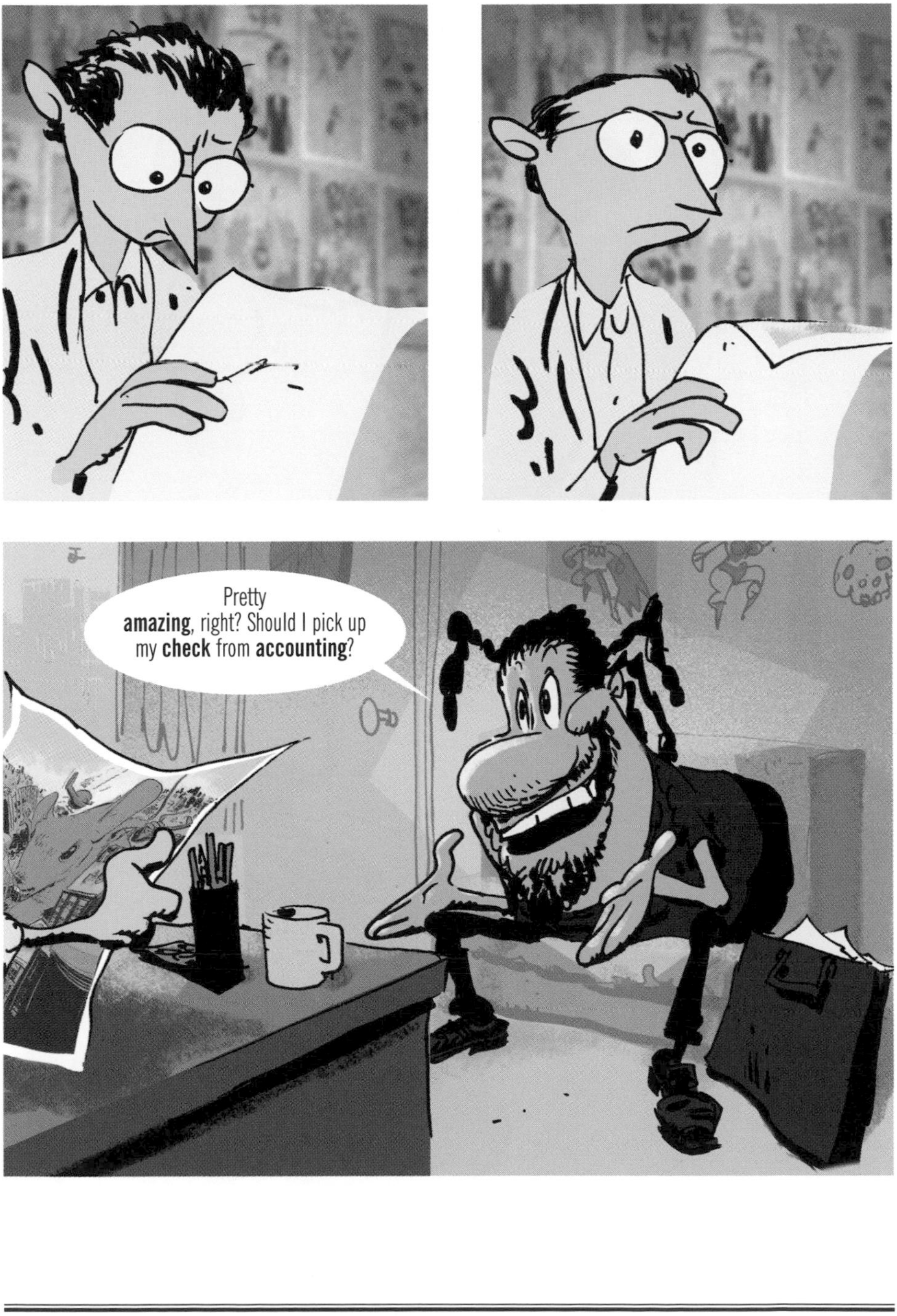
Pretty **amazing**, right? Should I pick up my **check** from **accounting**?

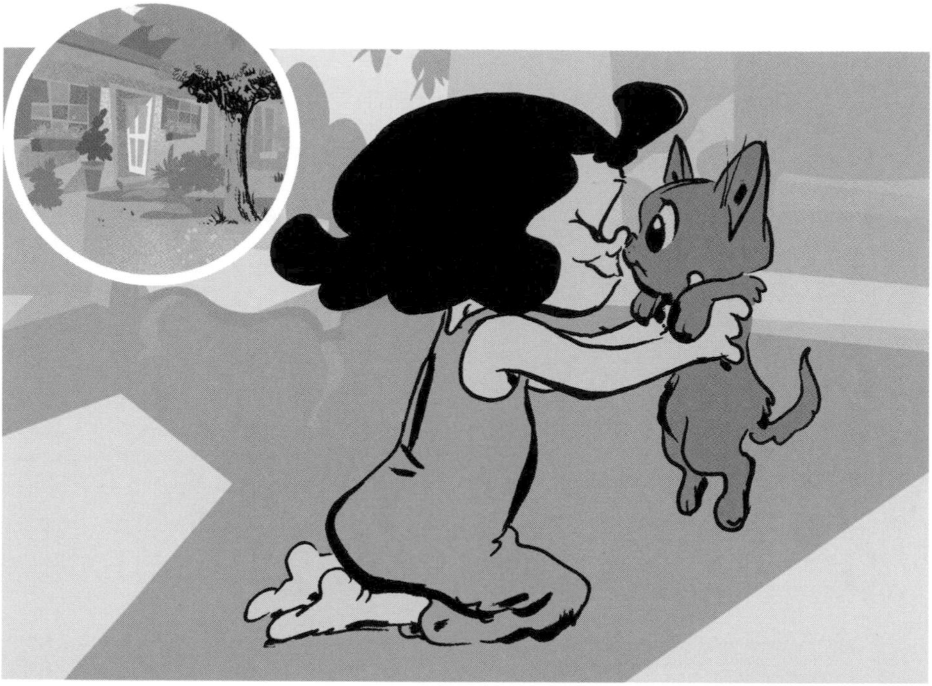

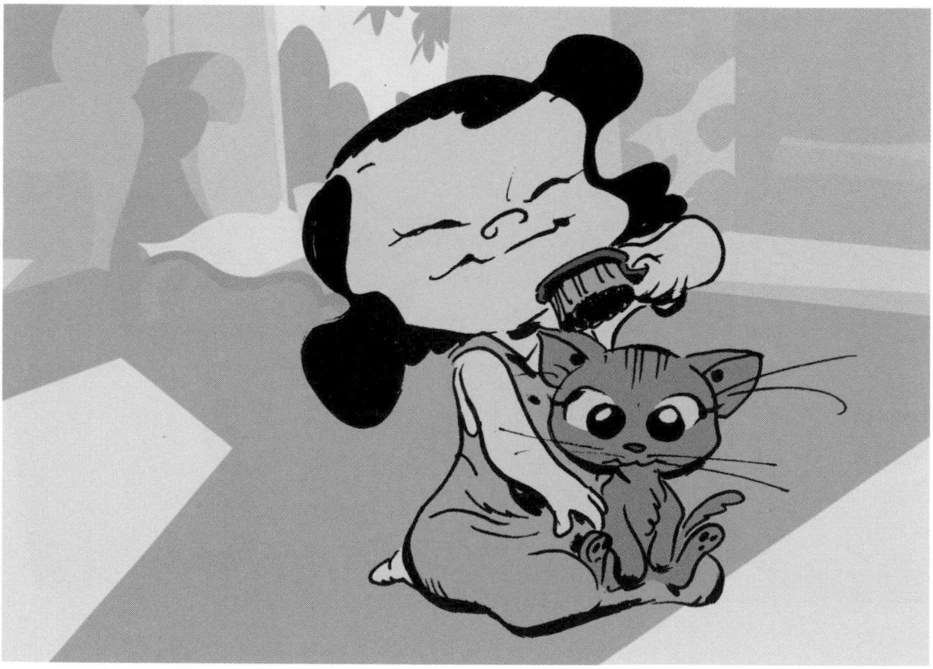

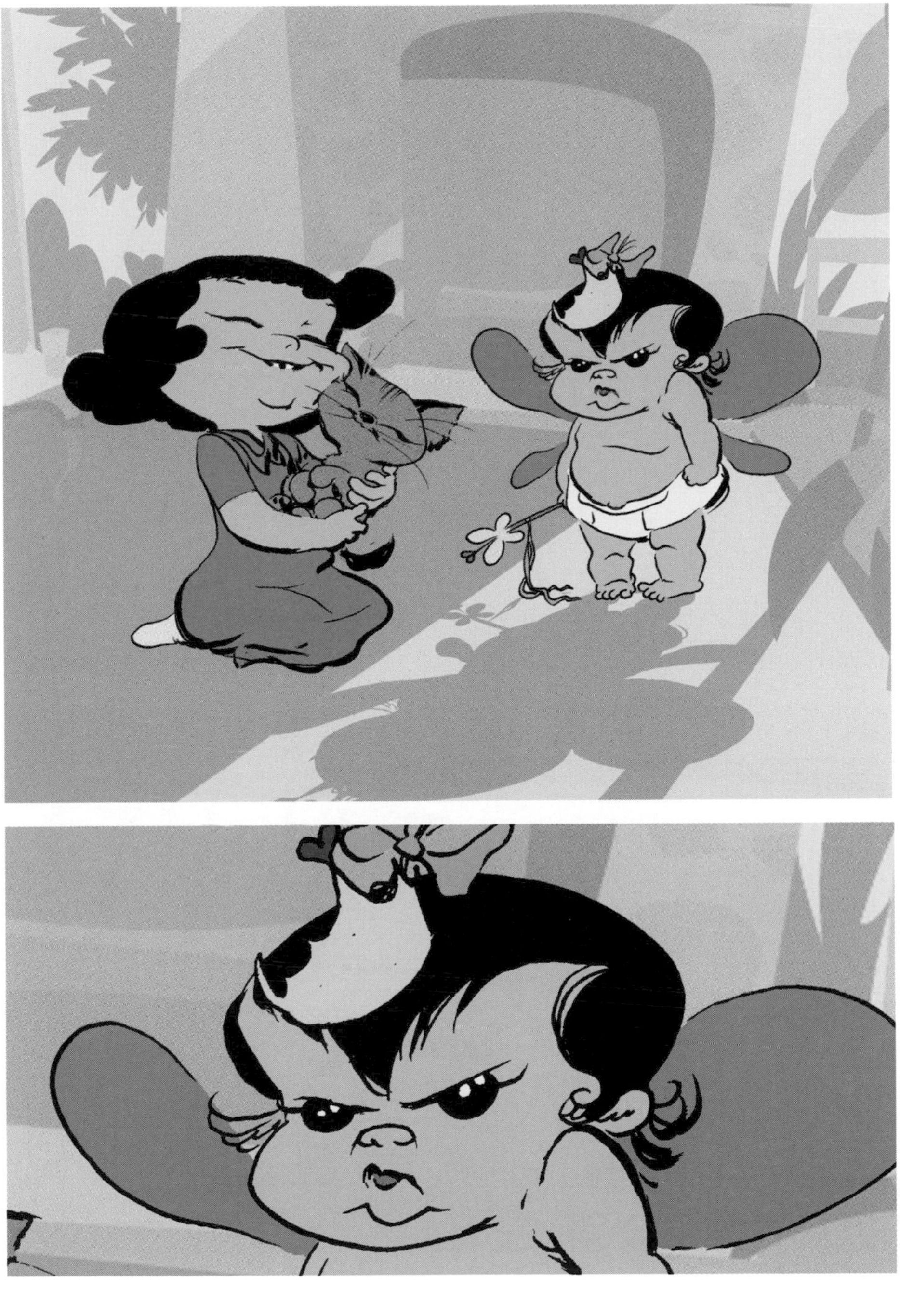

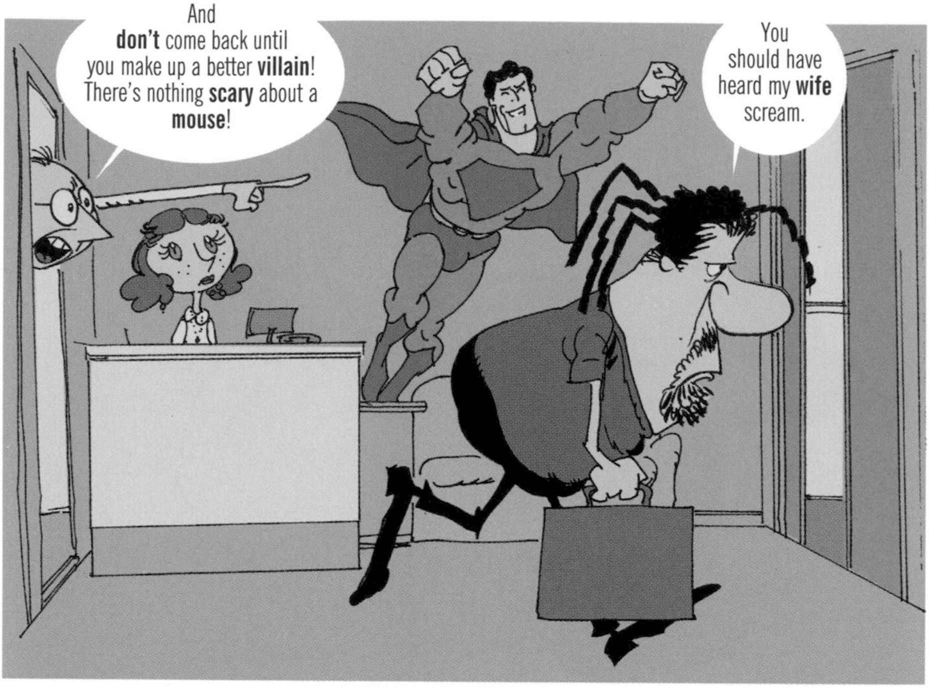
And **don't** come back until you make up a better **villain**! There's nothing **scary** about a **mouse**!
You should have heard my **wife** scream.

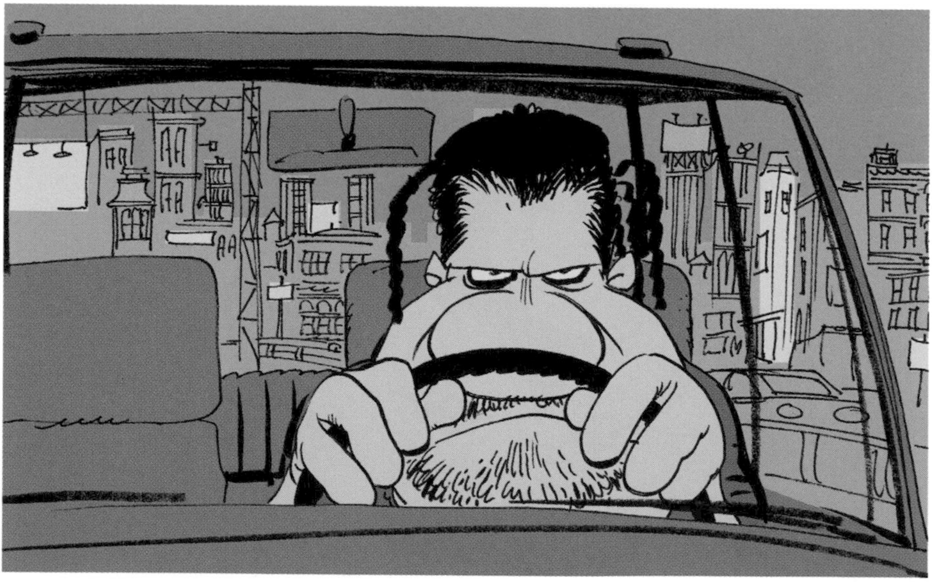

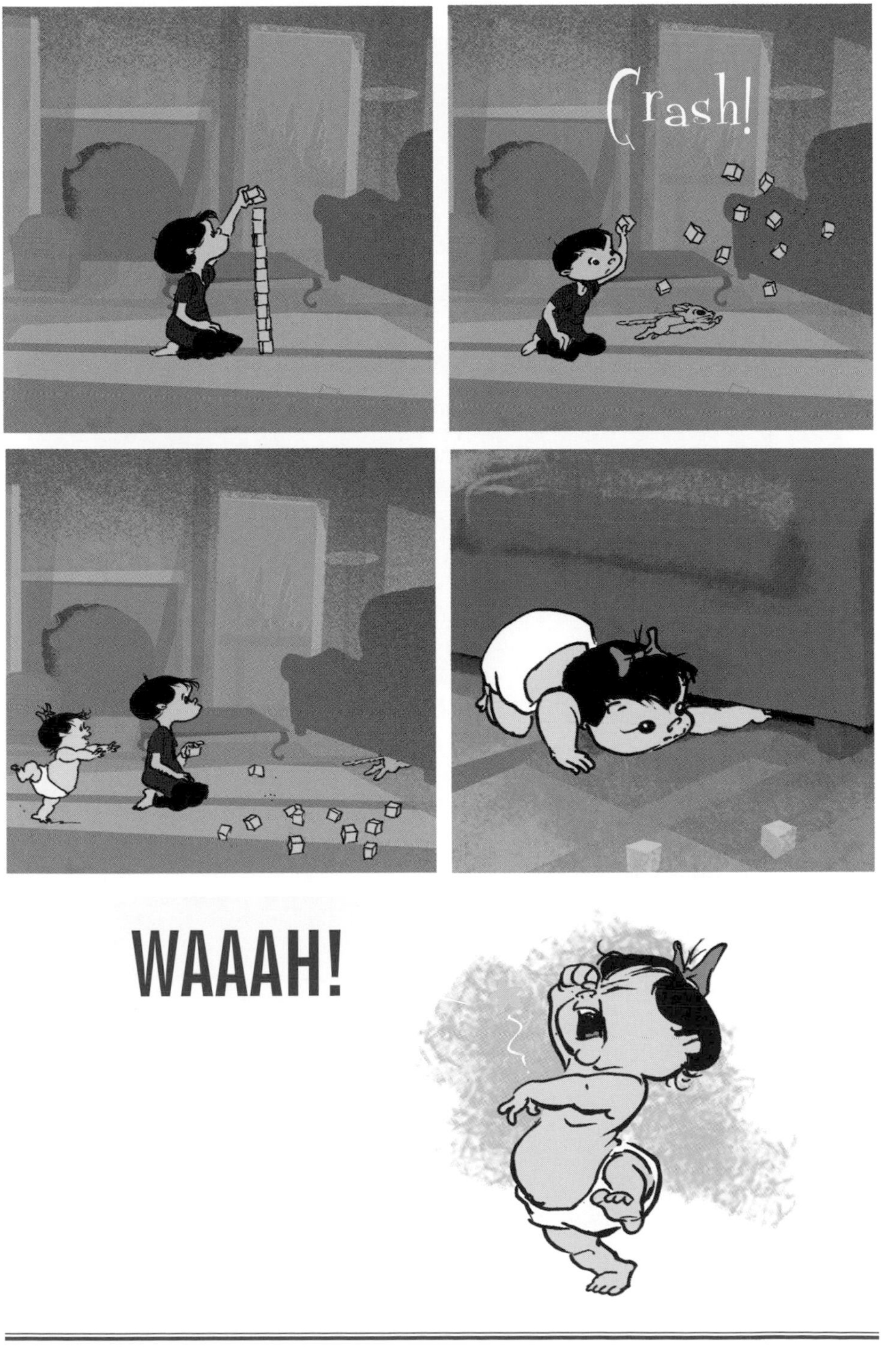
Crash!
WAAAH!

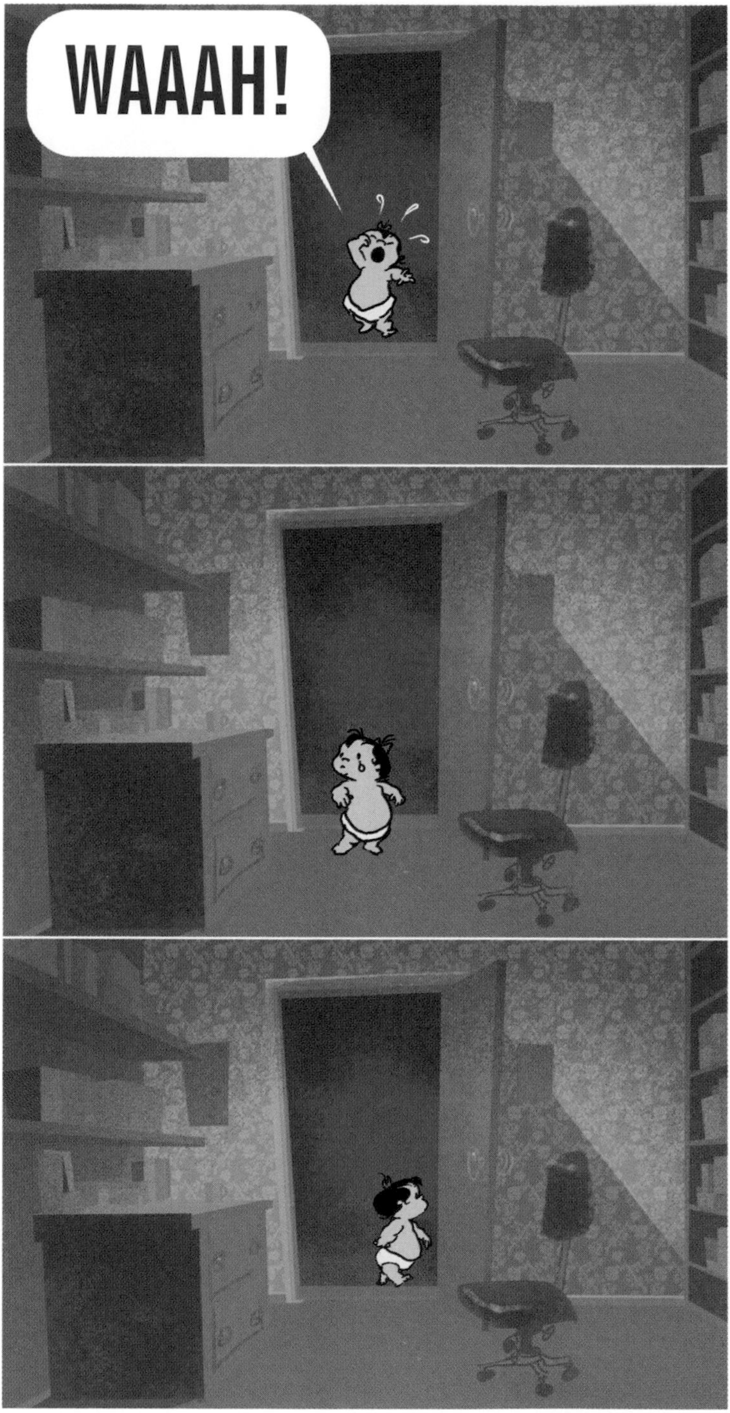
WAAAH!

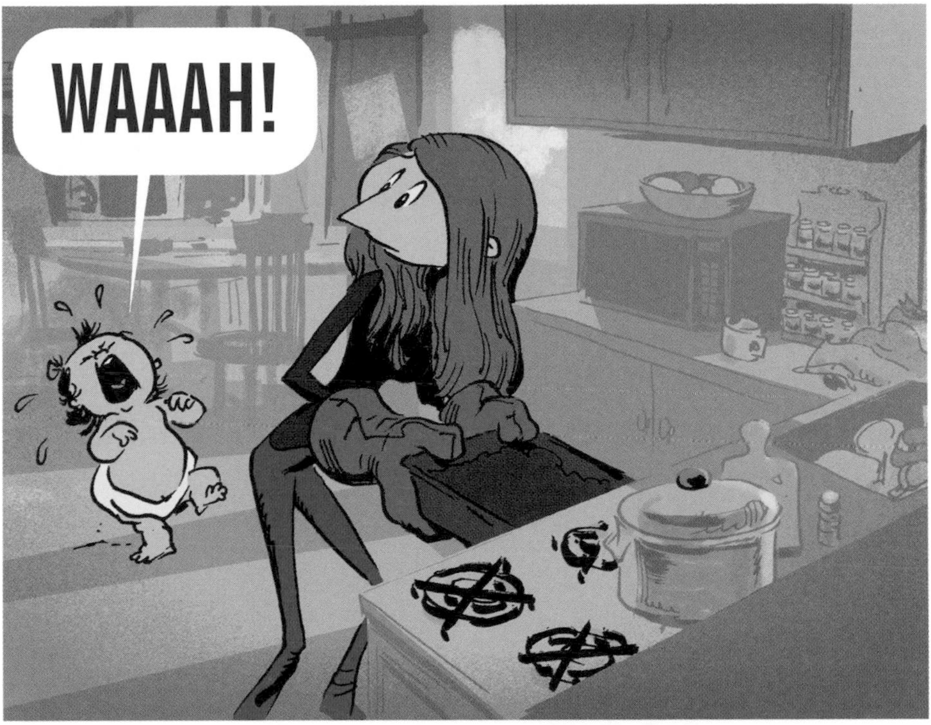
WAAAH!

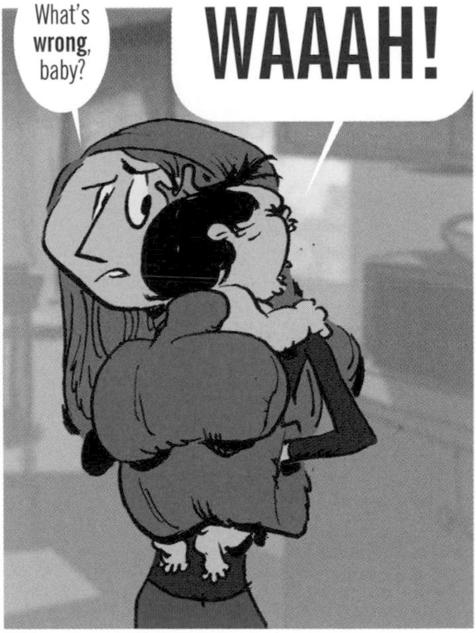
What's **wrong**, baby?
WAAAH!

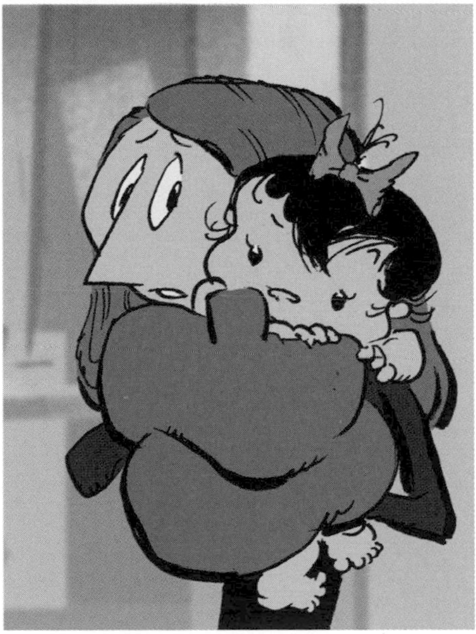

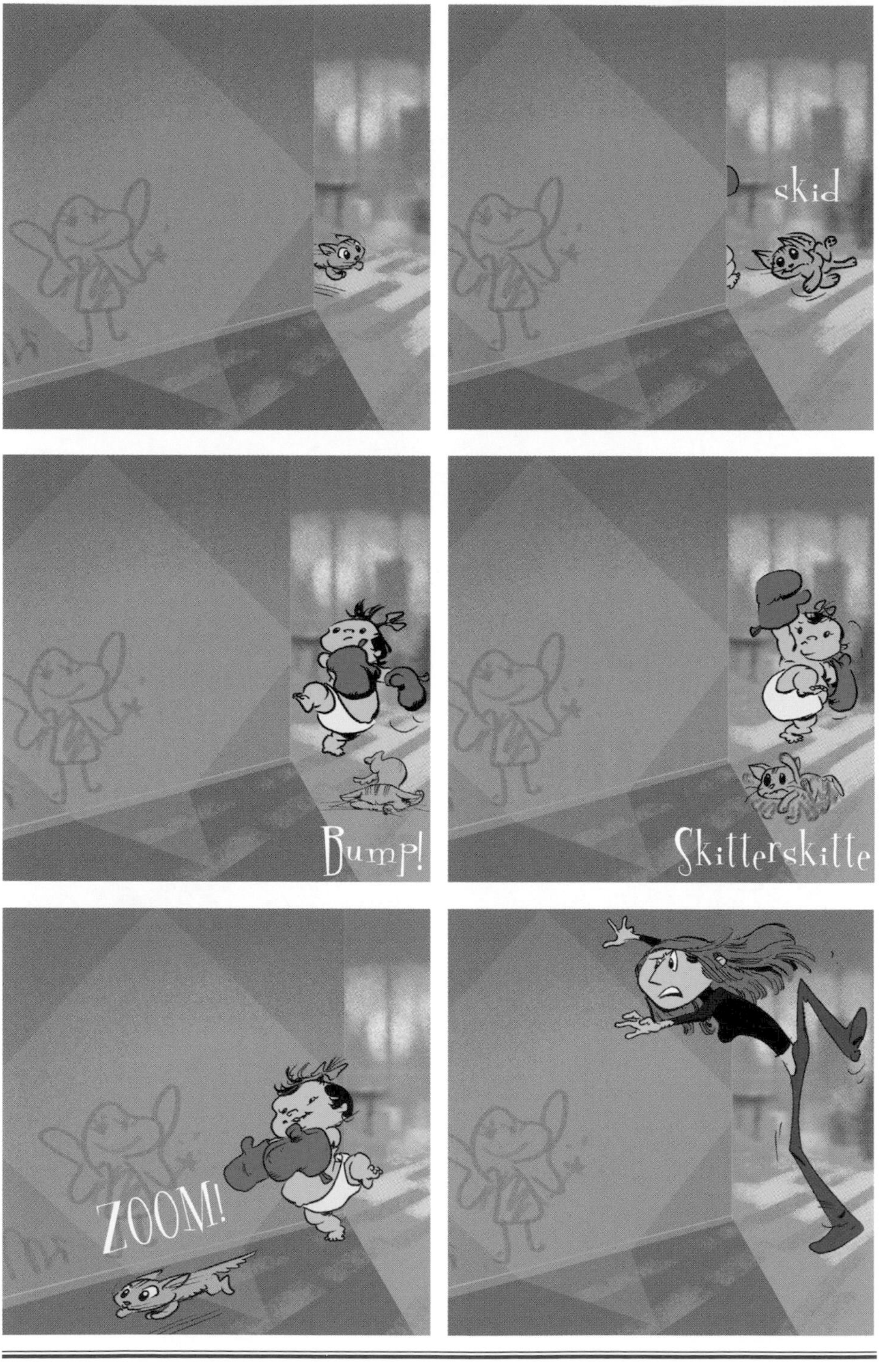
skid
Bump!
Skitterskitte
ZOOM!

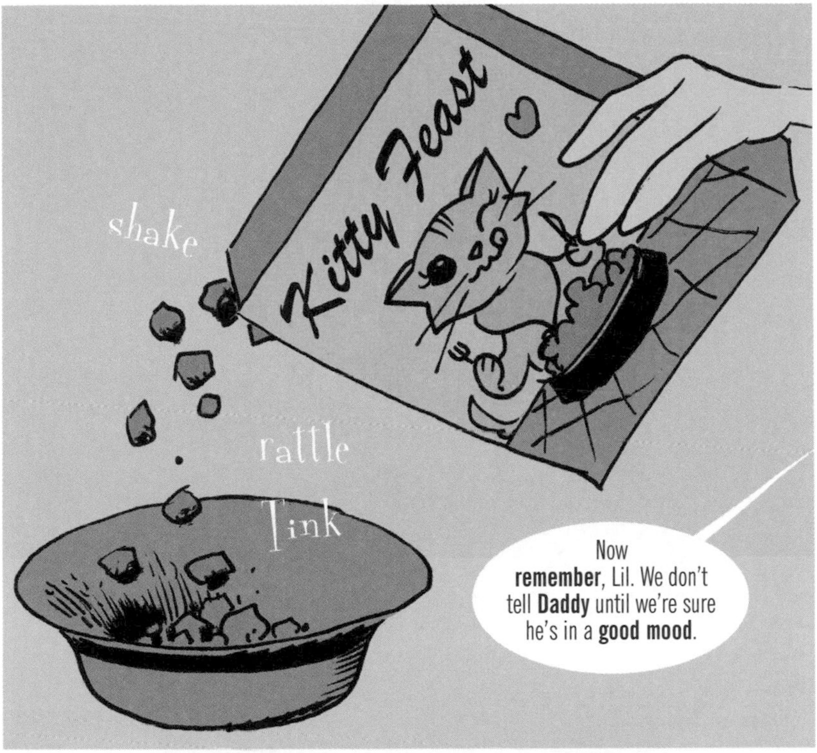
Kitty Feast
shake
rattle
Tink
Now **remember**, Lil. We don't tell **Daddy** until we're sure he's in a **good mood**.

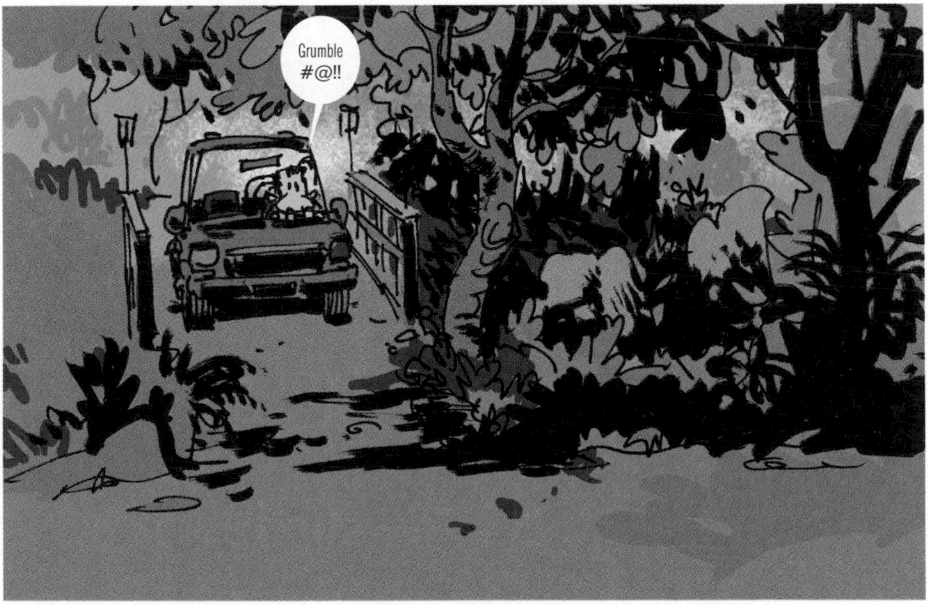
Grumble #@!!

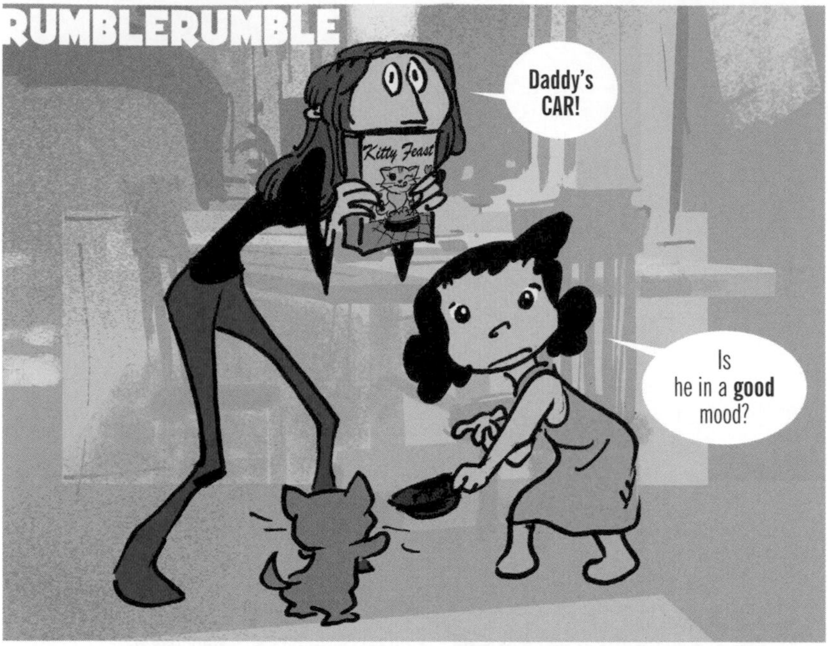
RUMBLERUMBLE
Kitty Feast
Daddy's CAR!
Is he in a **good** mood?

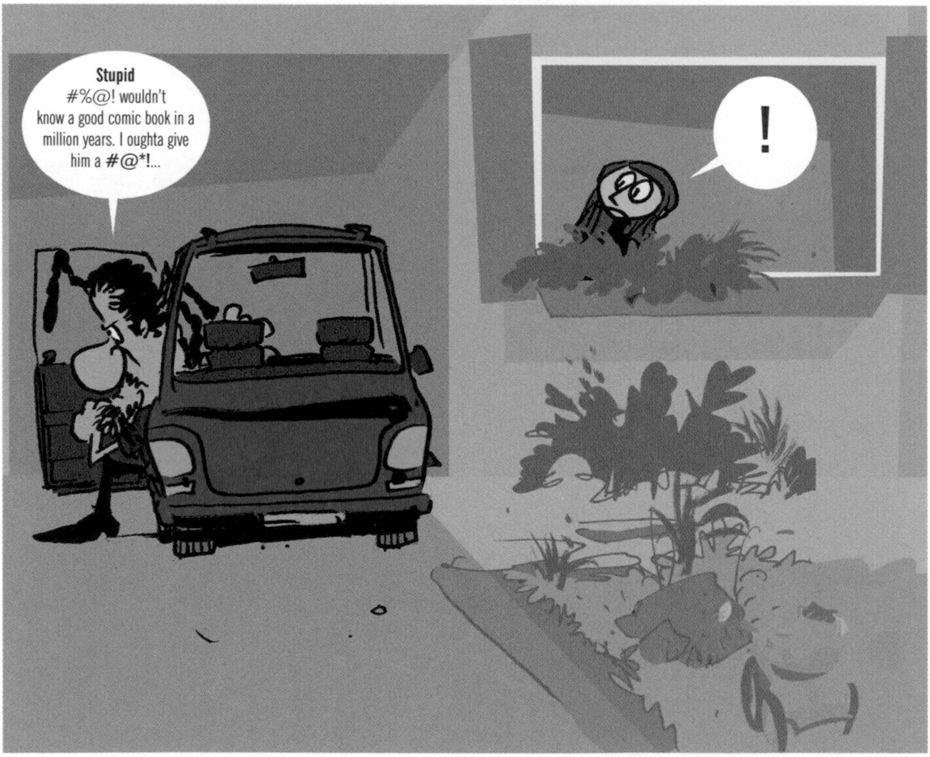
Stupid #%@! wouldn't know a good comic book in a million years. I oughta give him a **#@*!**...
!

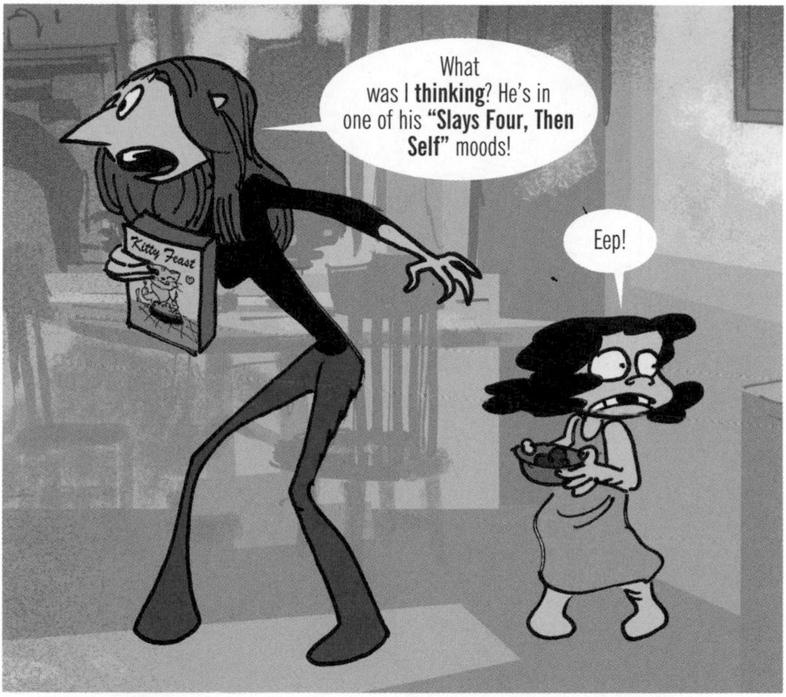
What was I **thinking**? He's in one of his **"Slays Four, Then Self"** moods!
Eep!
Kitty Feast
Kitty Feast

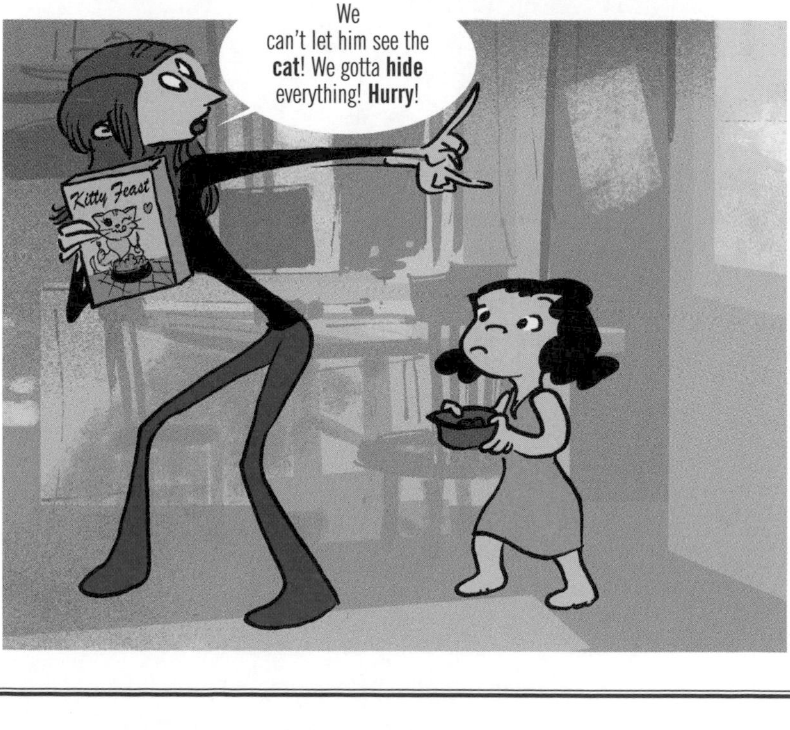
We can't let him see the **cat**! We gotta **hide** everything! **Hurry**!
Kitty Feast

Kitty Feast
That's the first place he **always** goes!
Kitty Feast

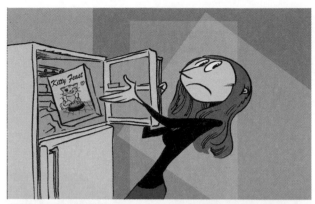

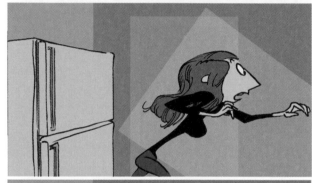

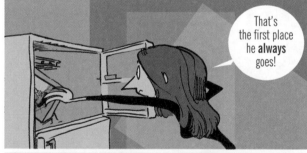

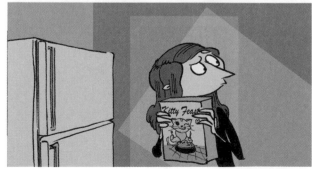

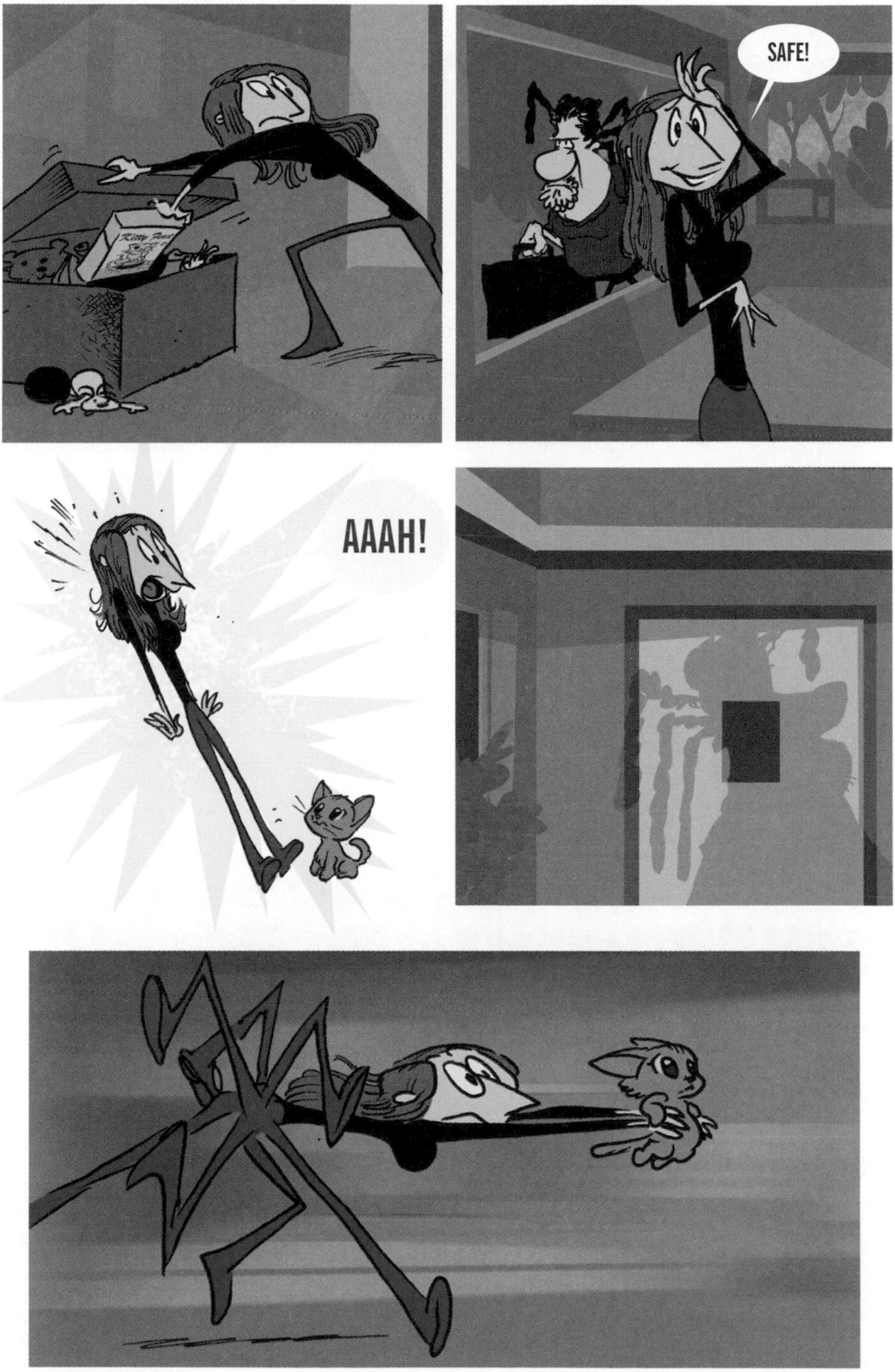
SAFE!
AAAH!

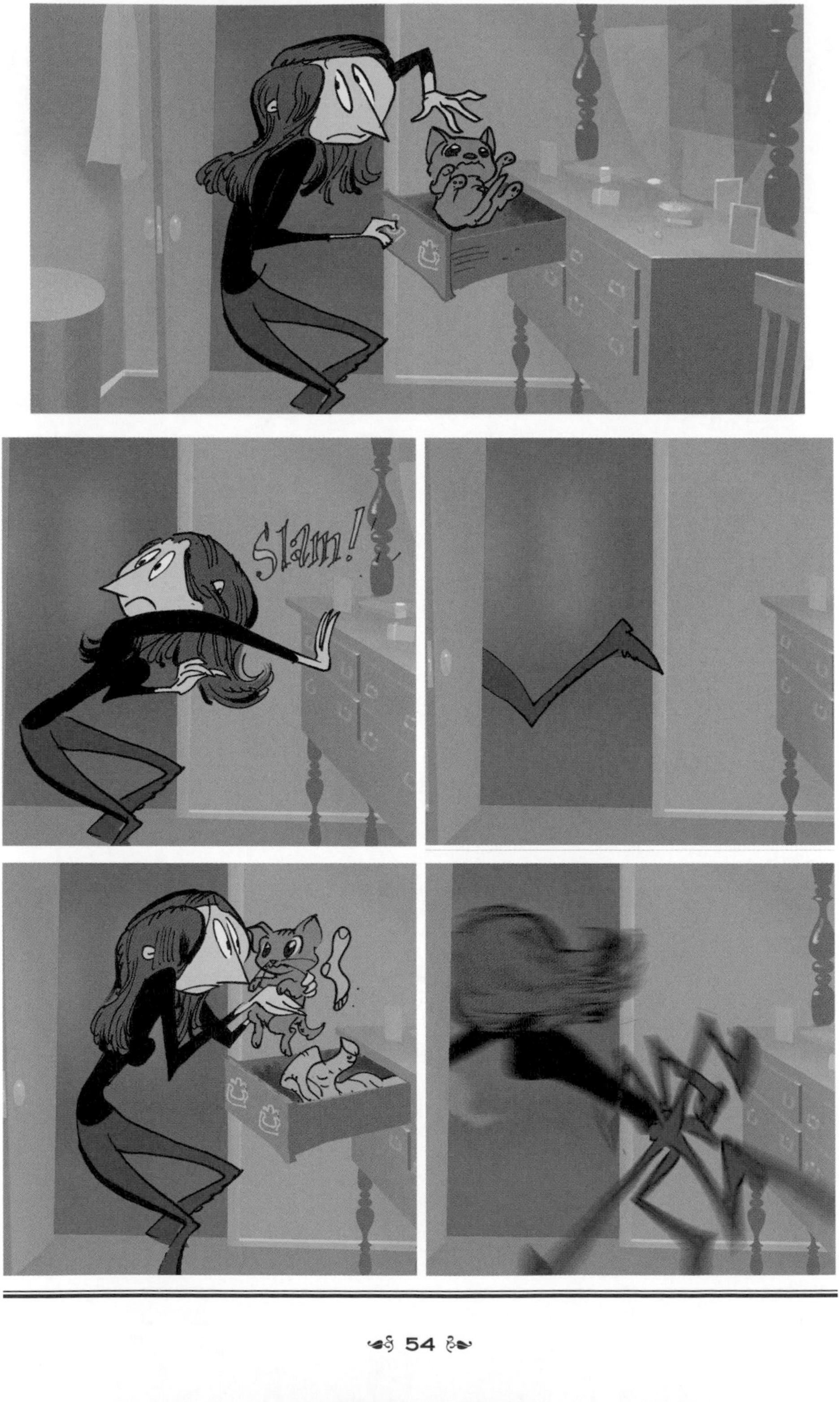
Slam!

Clatter
SMASH!

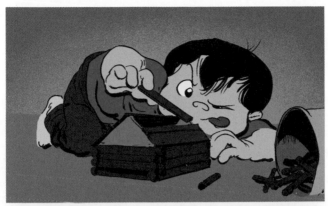

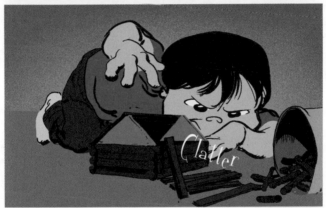

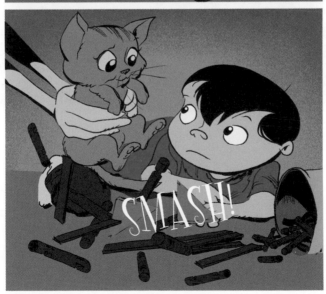

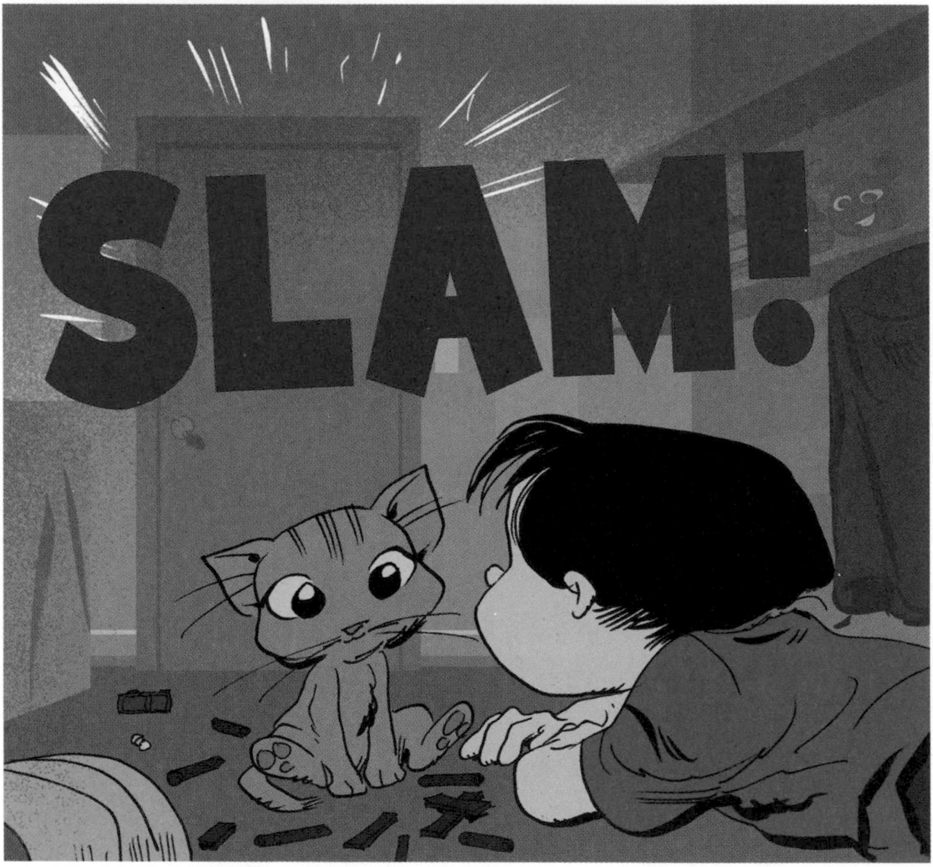
SLAM!

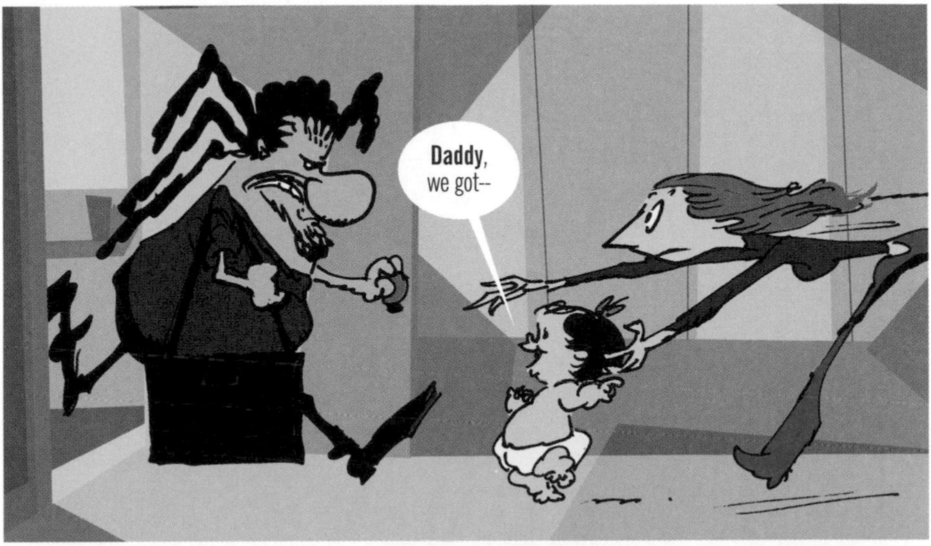
Daddy, we got--

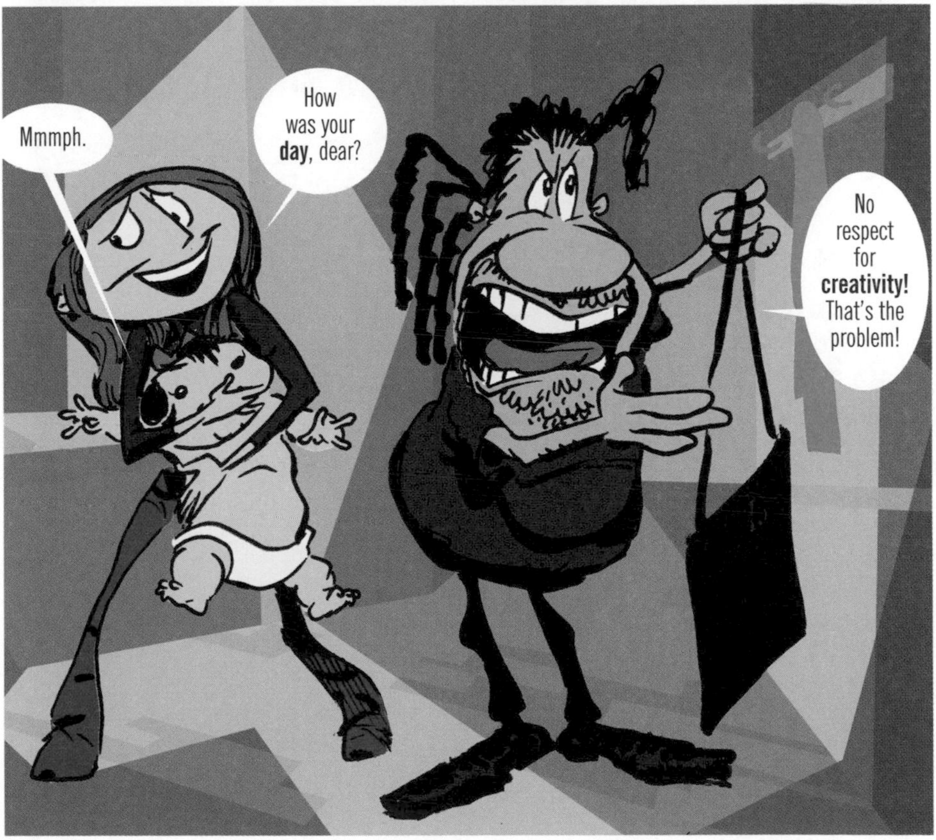
Mmmph.
How was your day, dear?
No respect for creativity! That's the problem!

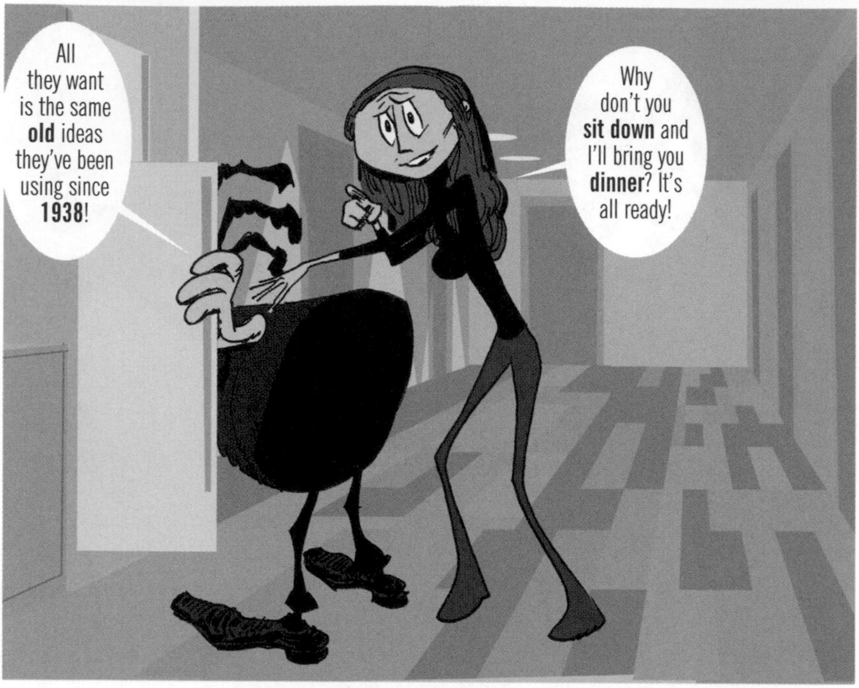
All they want is the same **old** ideas they've been using since **1938**!
Why don't you **sit down** and I'll bring you **dinner**? It's all ready!

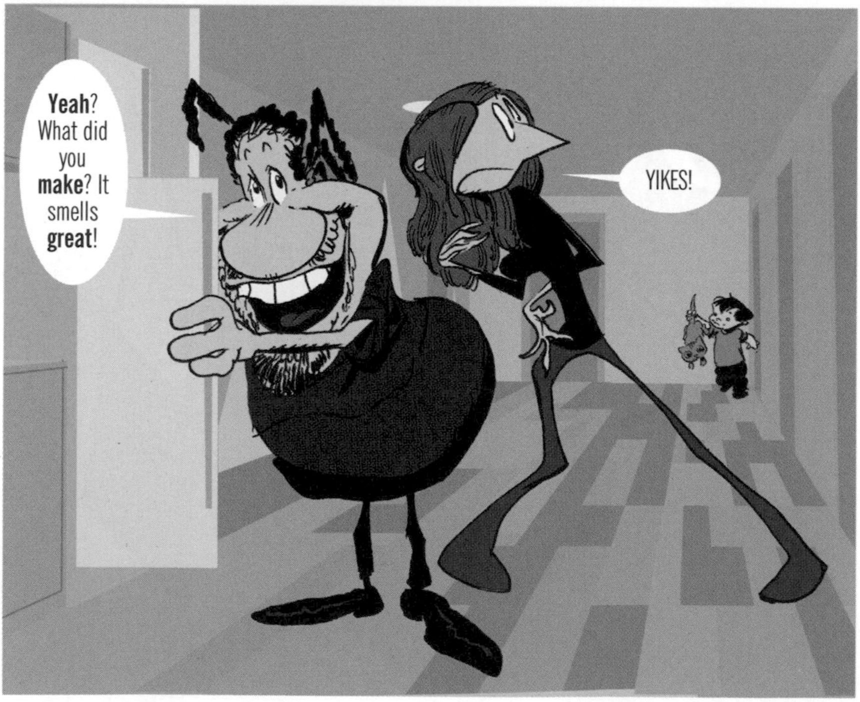
Yeah? What did you **make**? It smells **great**!
YIKES!

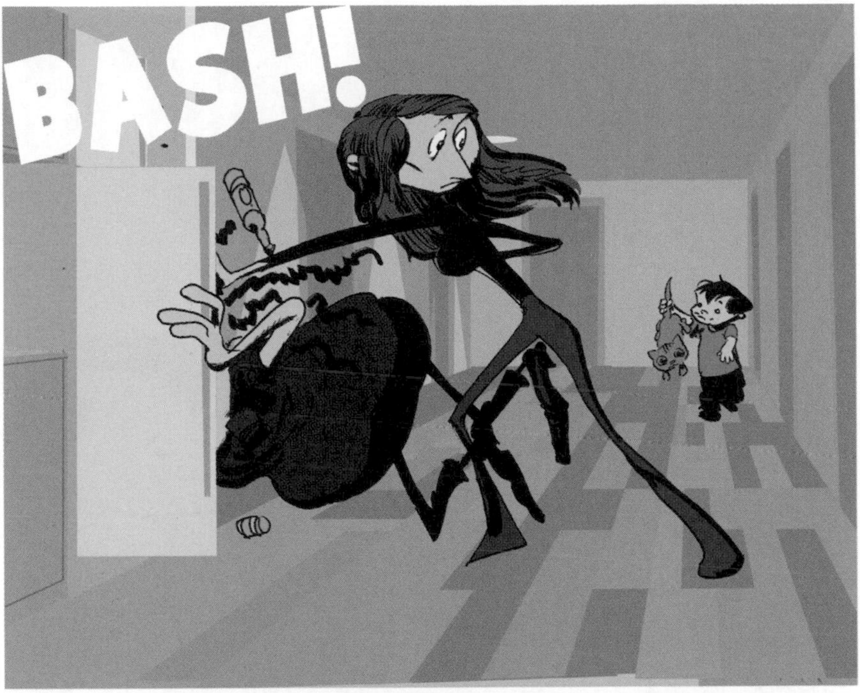
BASH!

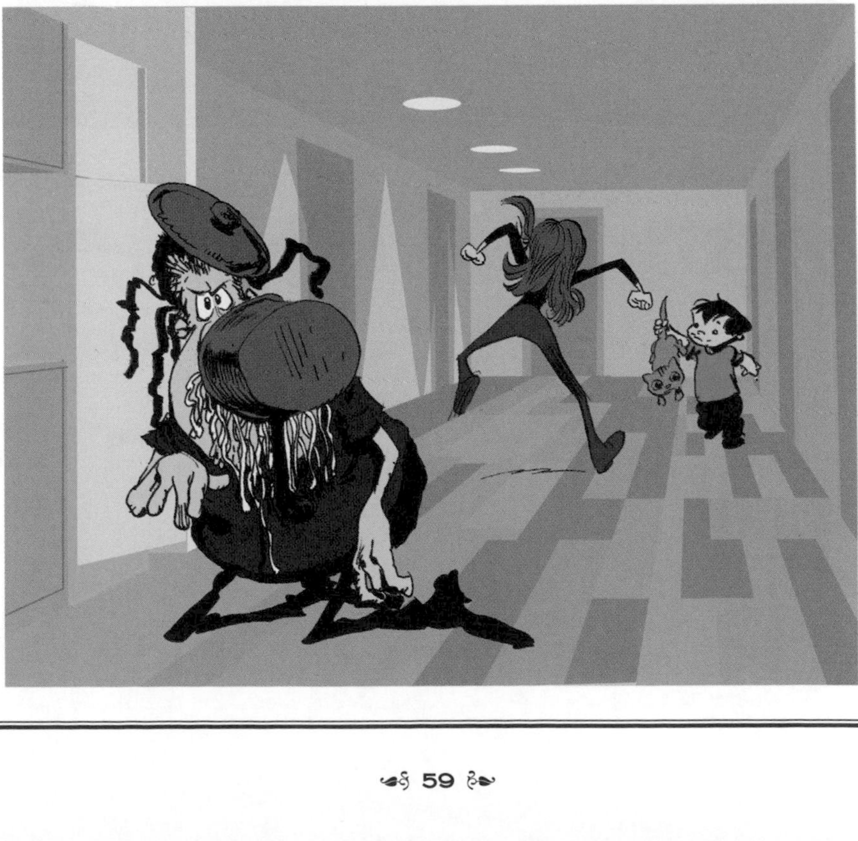

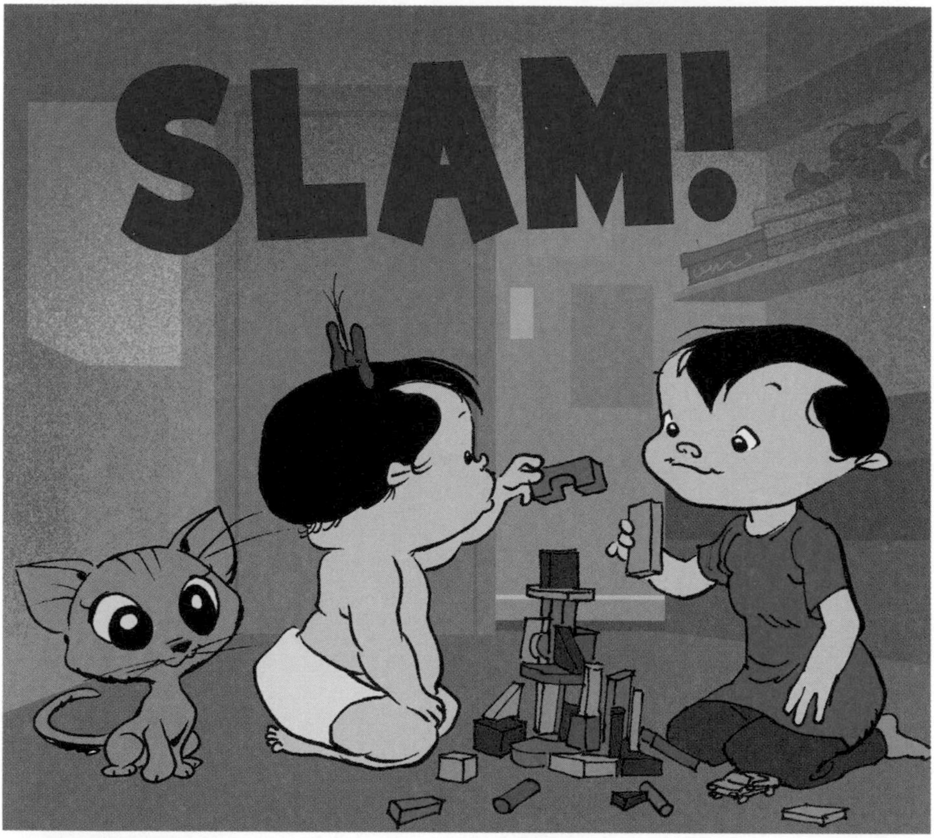
SLAM!

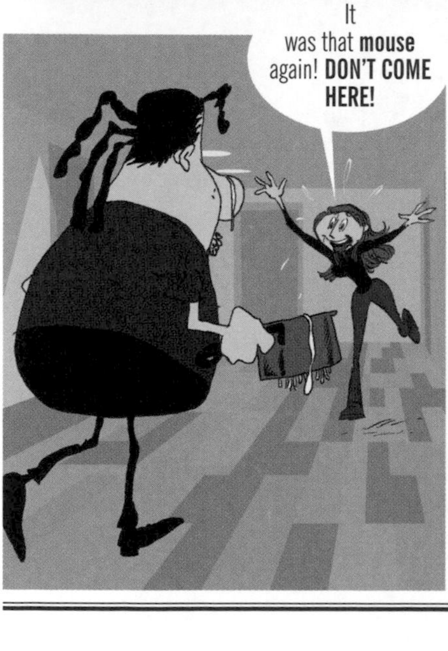
It was that **mouse** again! **DON'T COME HERE!**

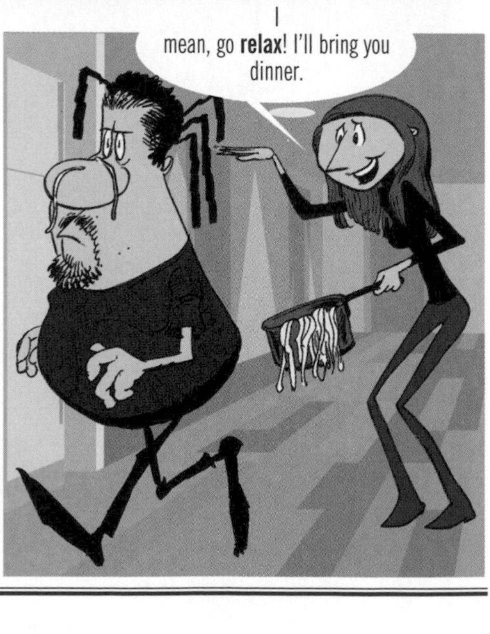
I mean, go **relax**! I'll bring you dinner.

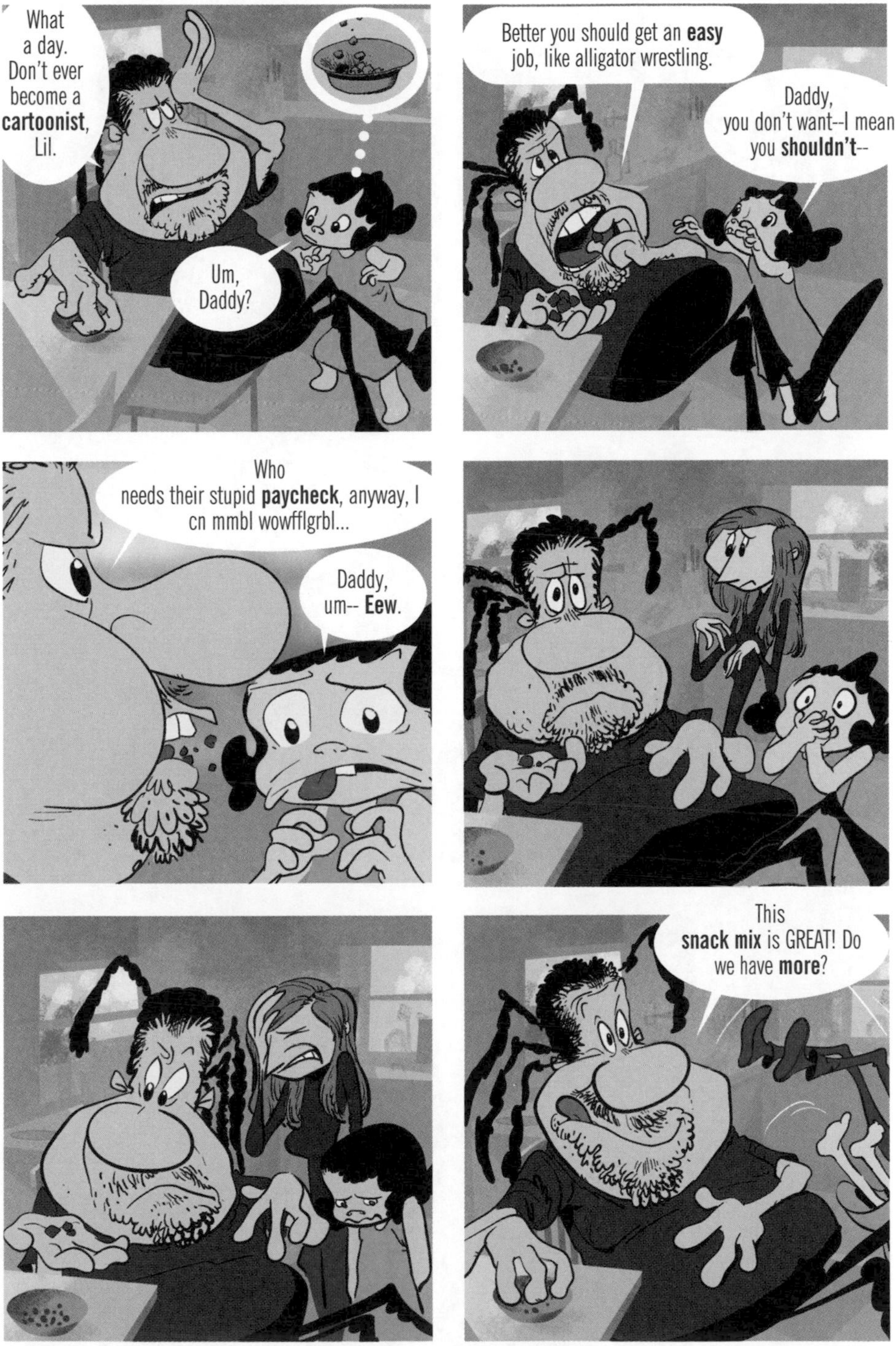
What a day. Don't ever become a **cartoonist**, Lil.
Um, Daddy?
Better you should get an **easy** job, like alligator wrestling.
Daddy, you don't want--I mean you **shouldn't**--
Who needs their stupid **paycheck**, anyway, I cn mmbl wowfflgrbl...
Daddy, um-- **Eew**.
This **snack mix** is GREAT! Do we have **more**?

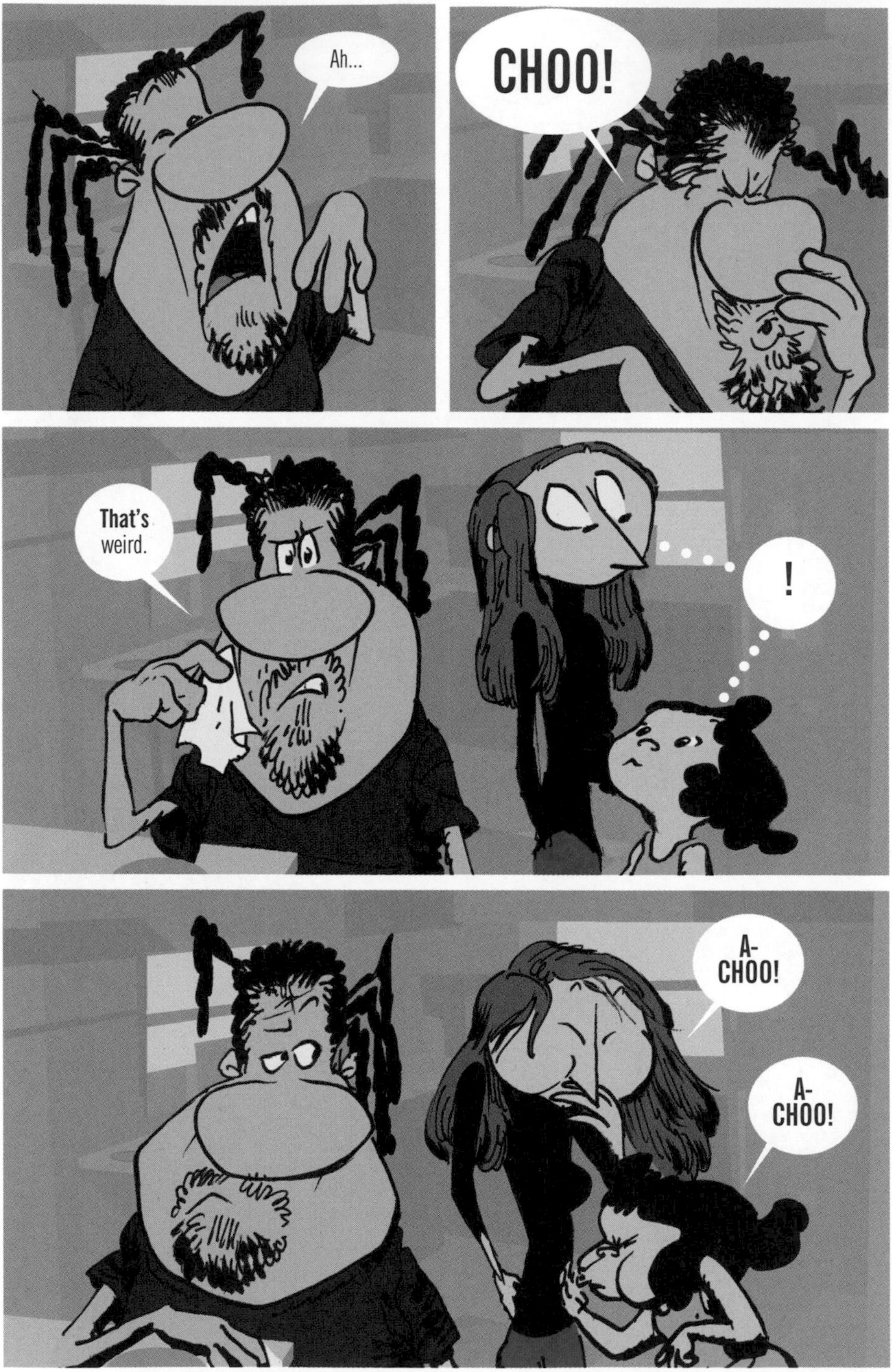
Ah...
CHOO!
That's weird.
!
A-CHOO!
A-CHOO!

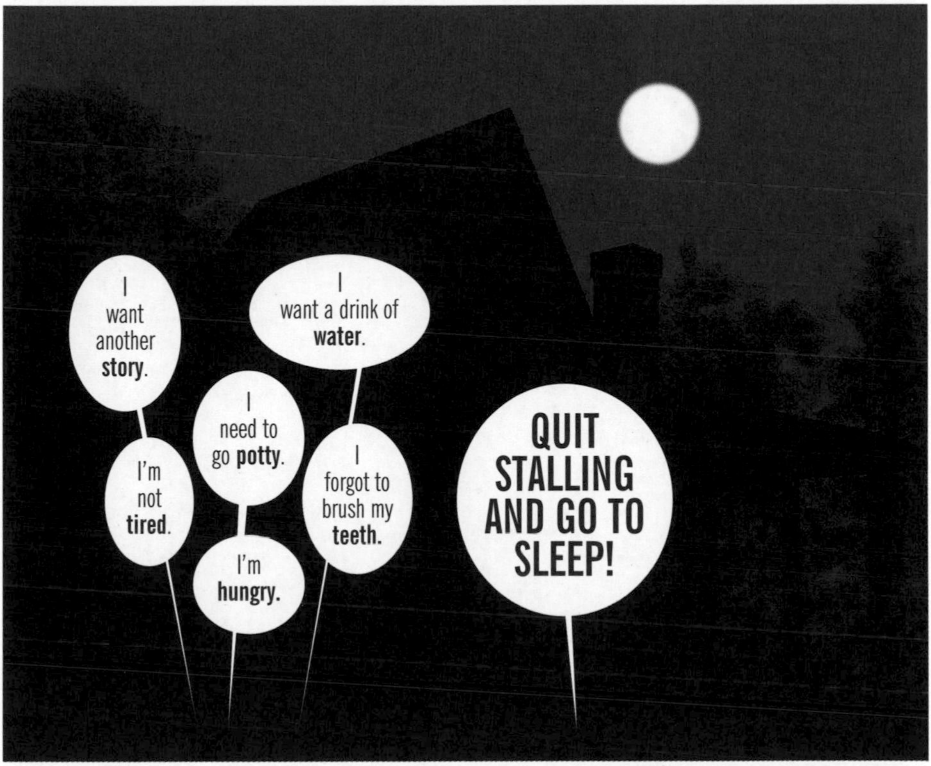
I want another **story**.
I'm not **tired**.
I need to go **potty**.
I'm **hungry**.
I want a drink of **water**.
I forgot to brush my **teeth**.
QUIT STALLING AND GO TO SLEEP!

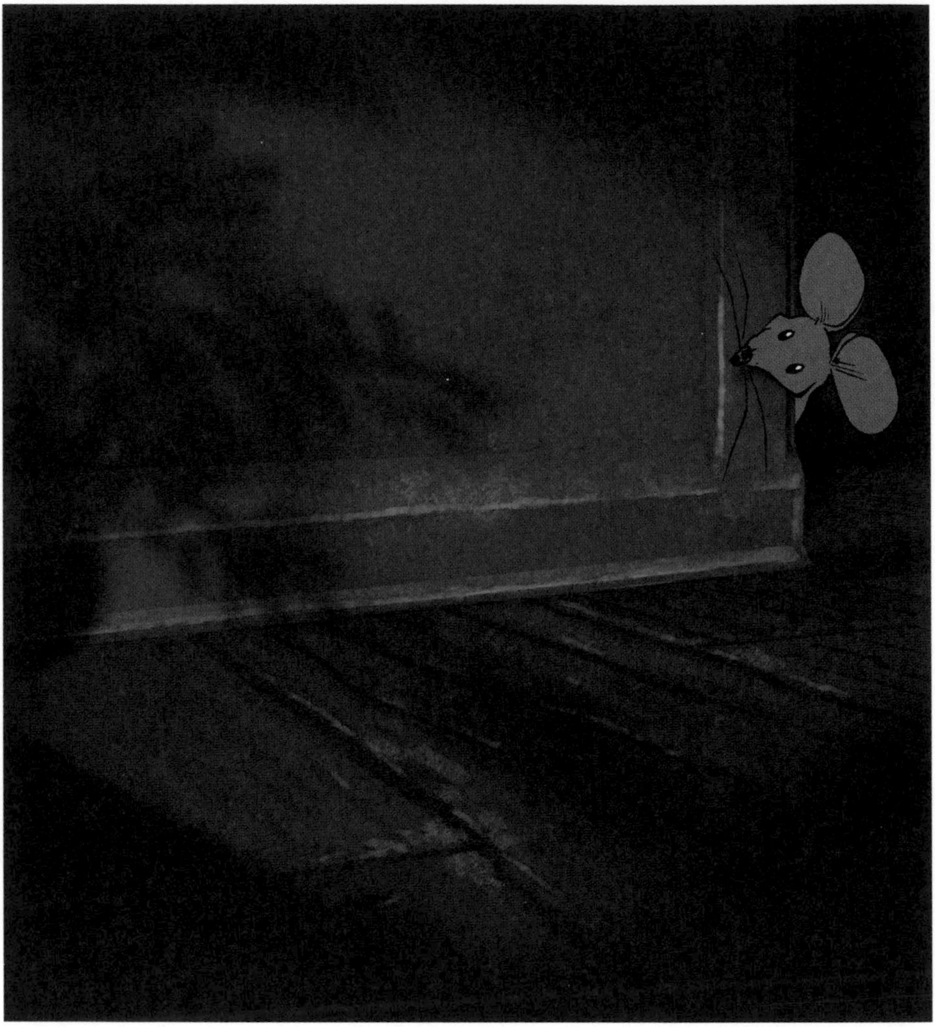

Skitterskitter

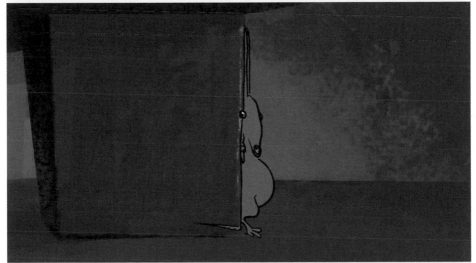

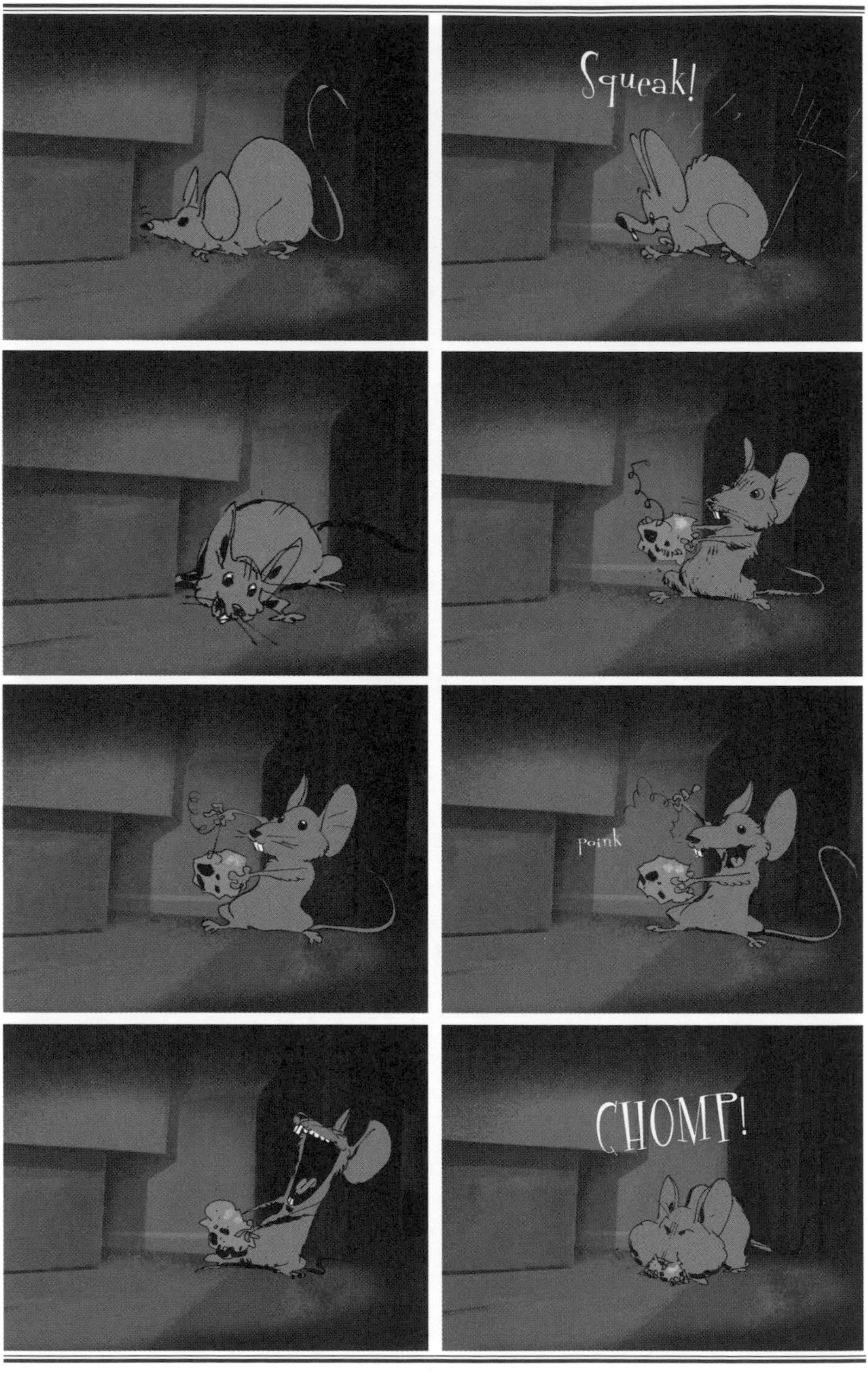
Squeak!
poink
CHOMP!

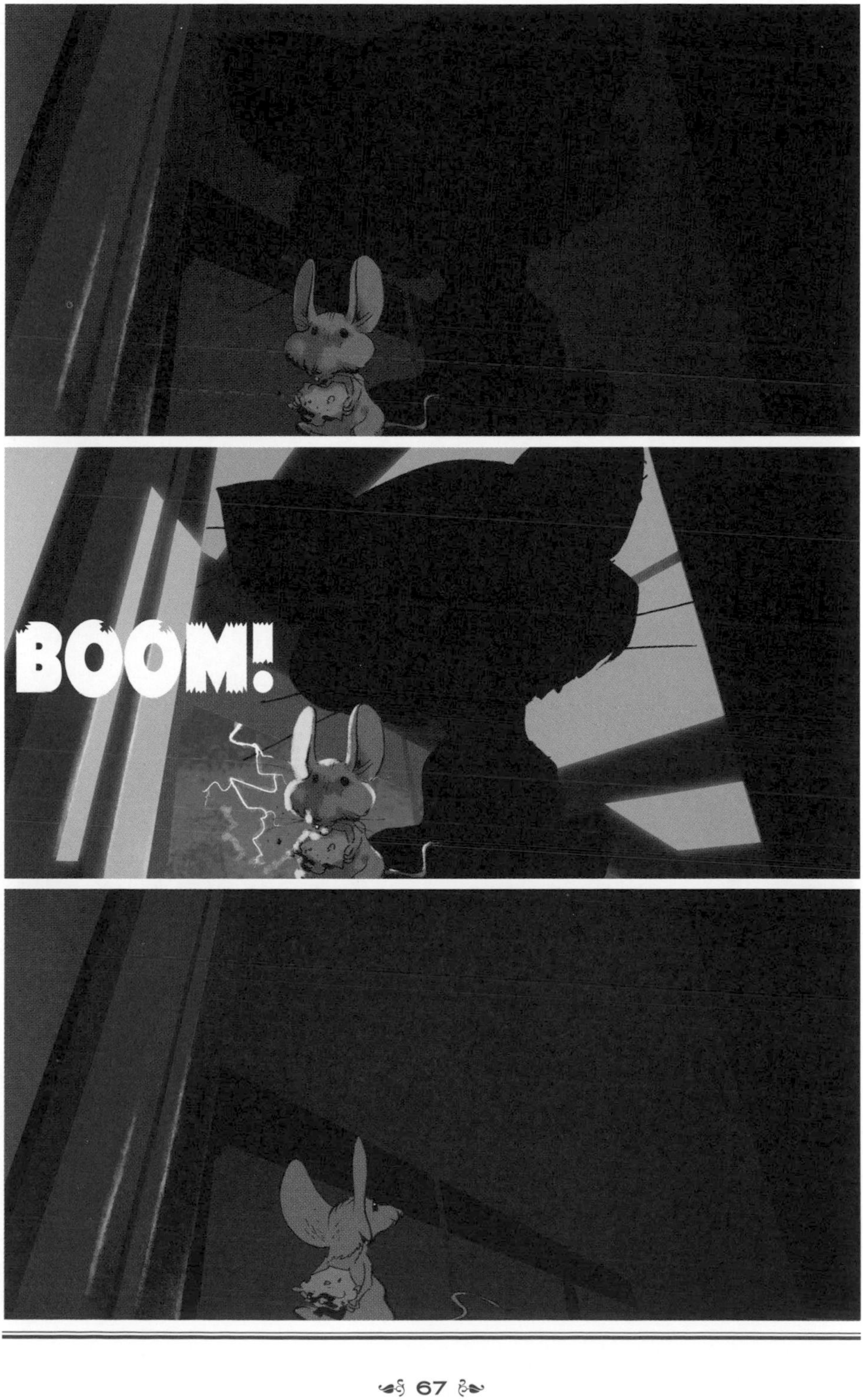
BOOM!

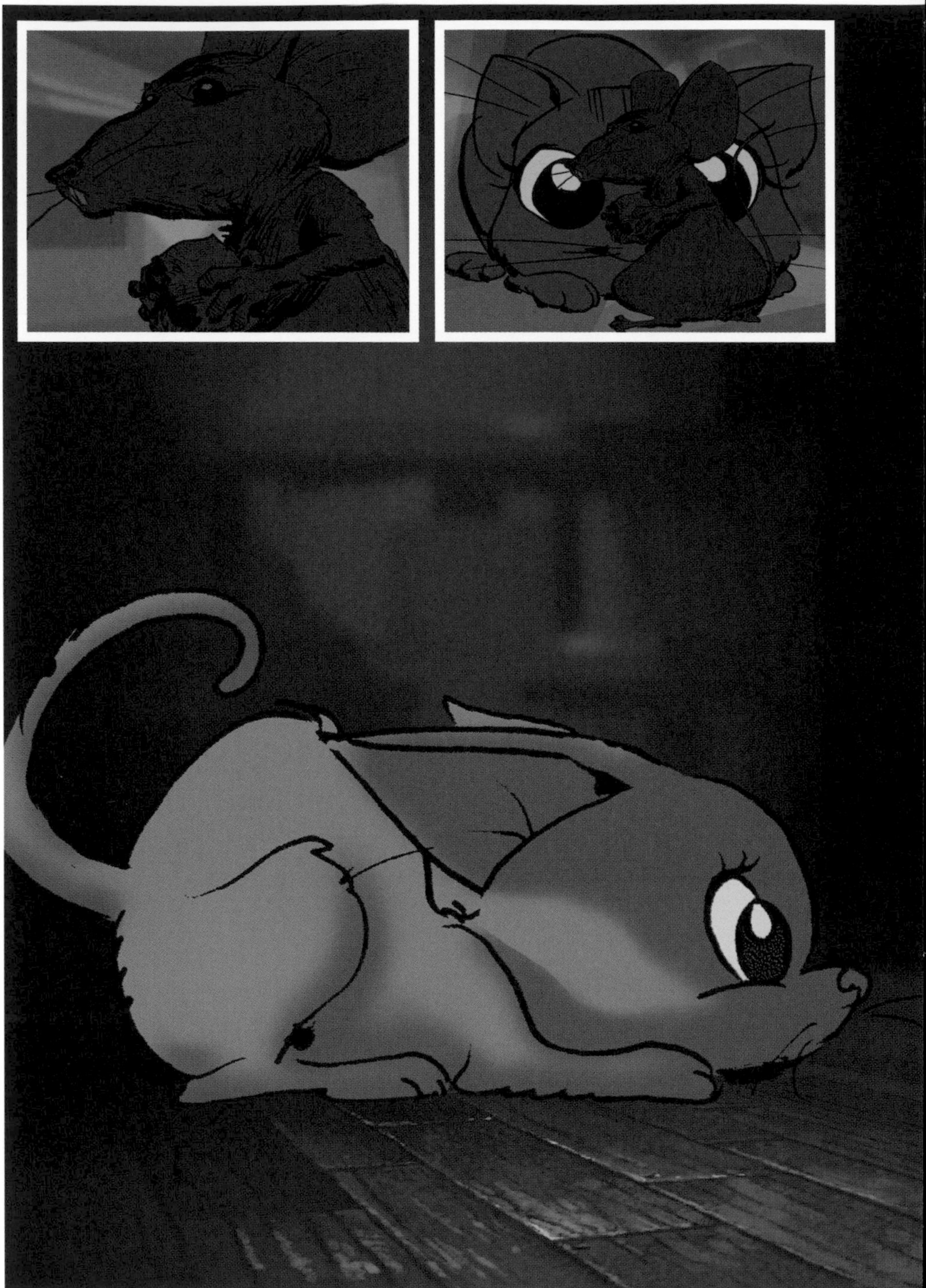

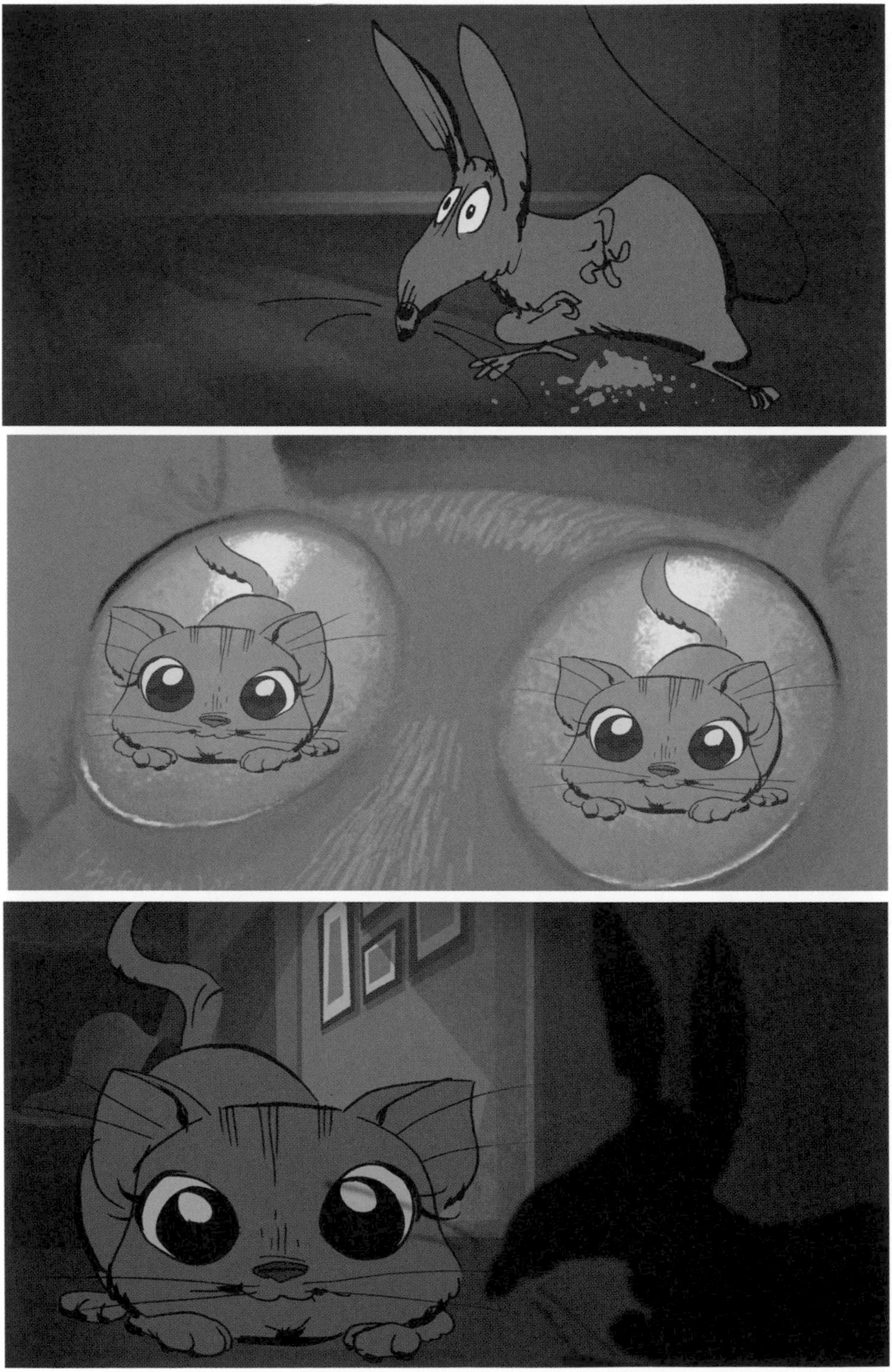

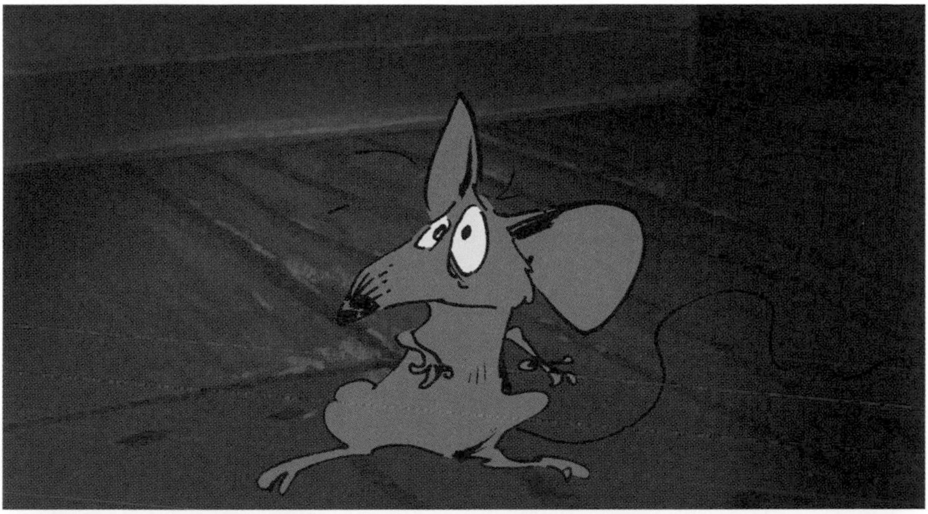

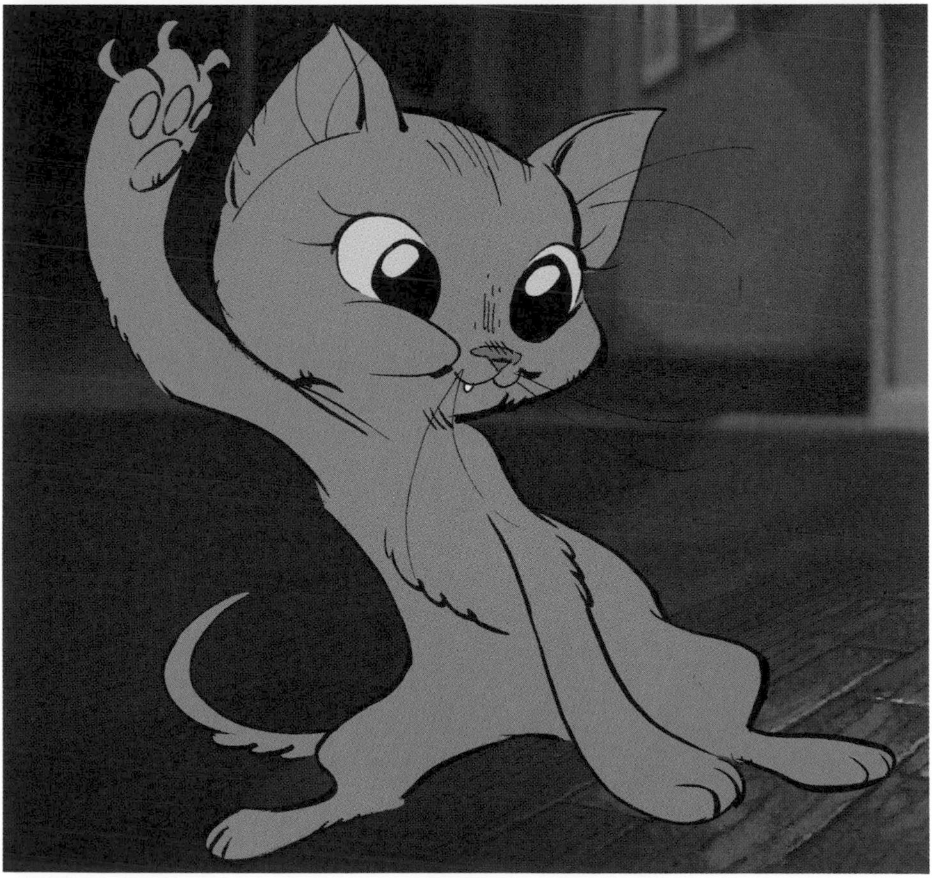

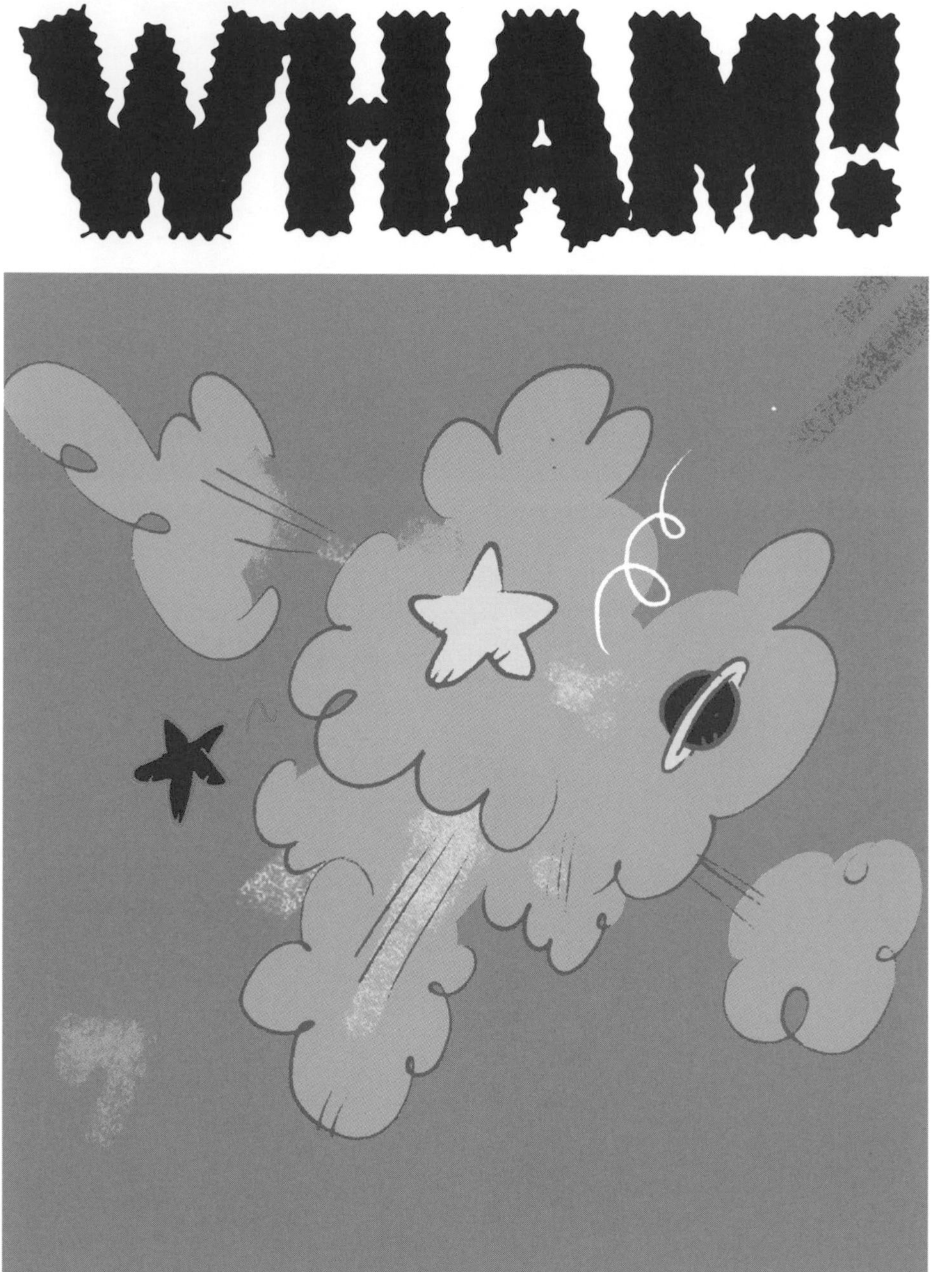
WHAM!

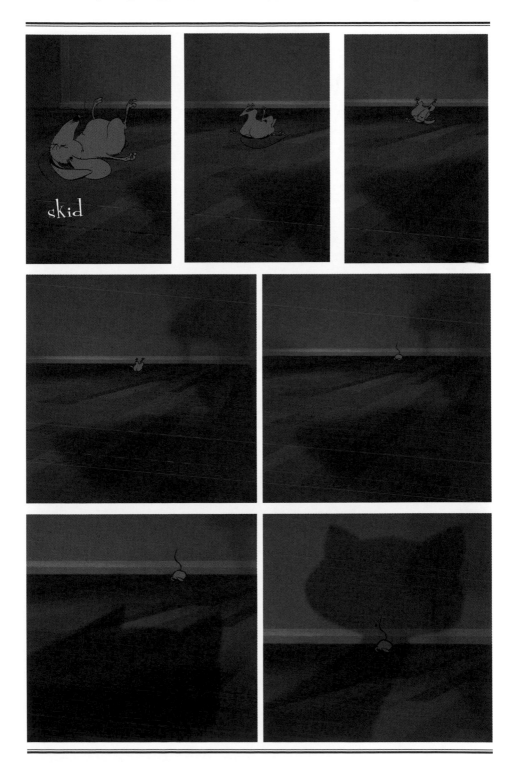

skid

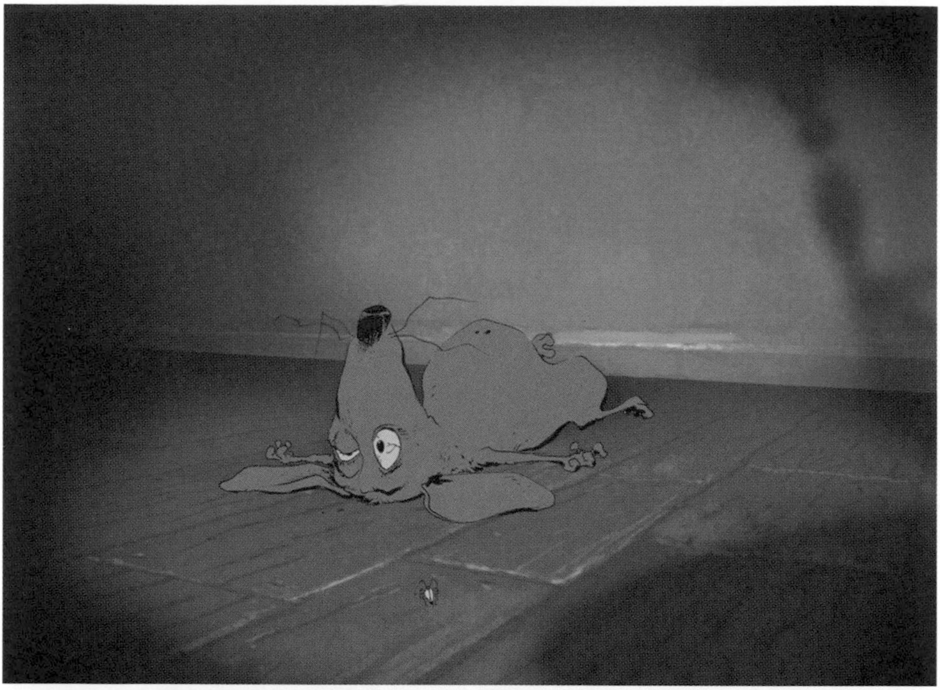

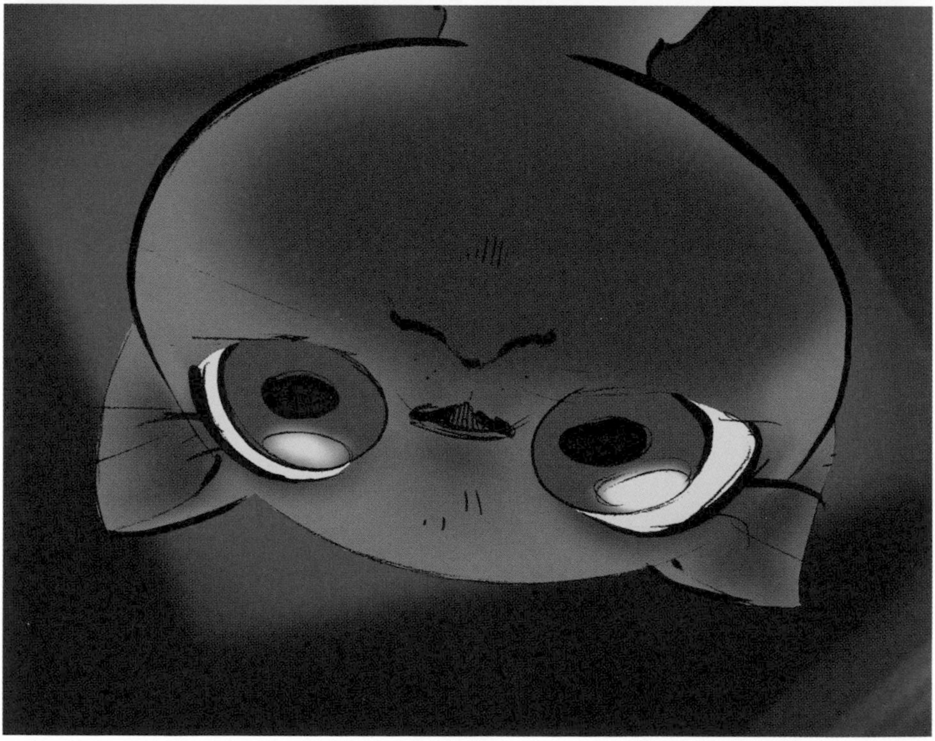

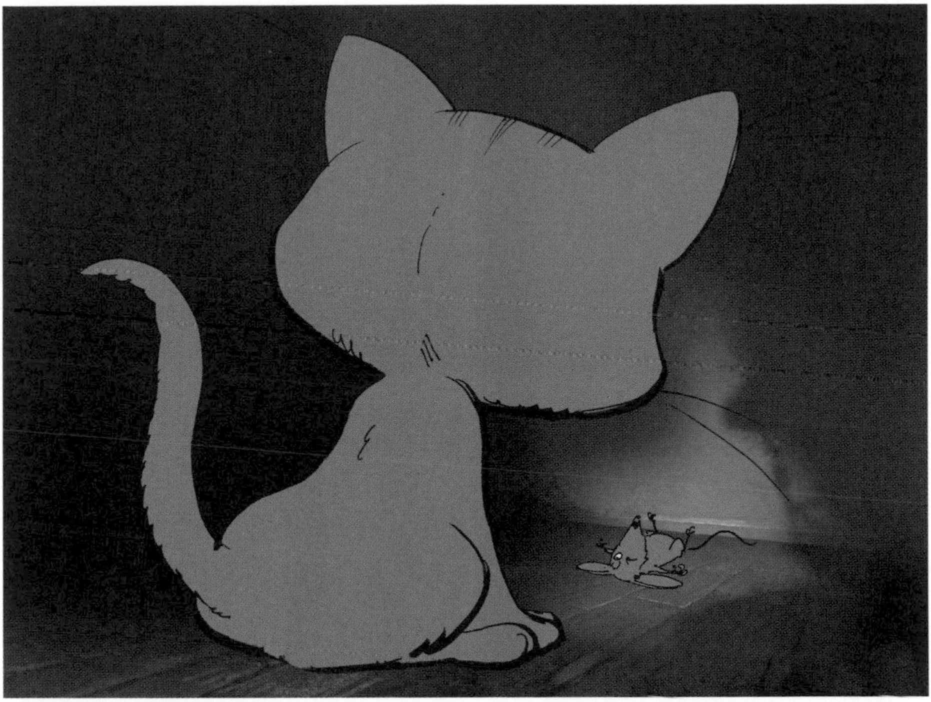

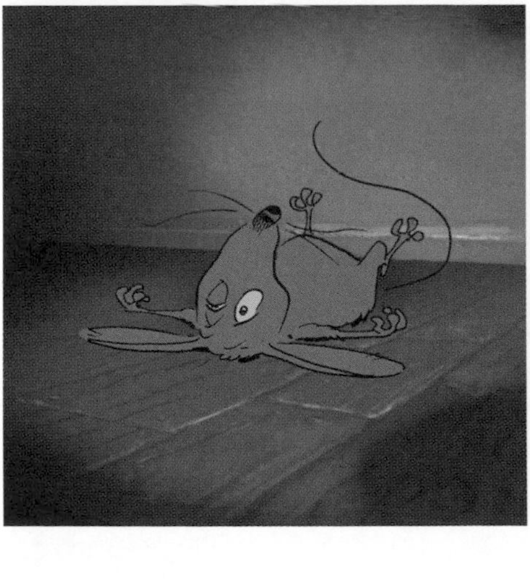

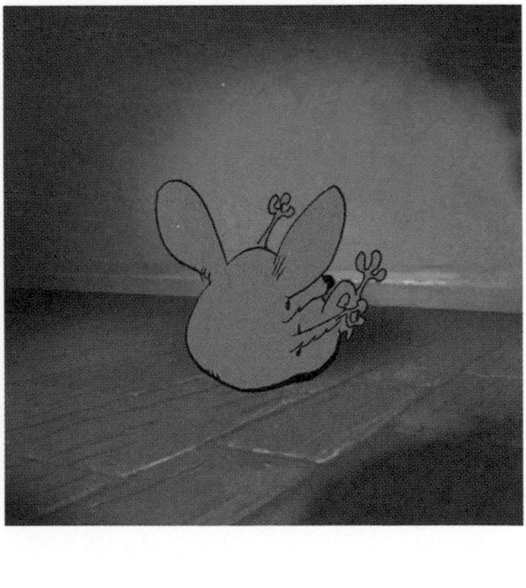

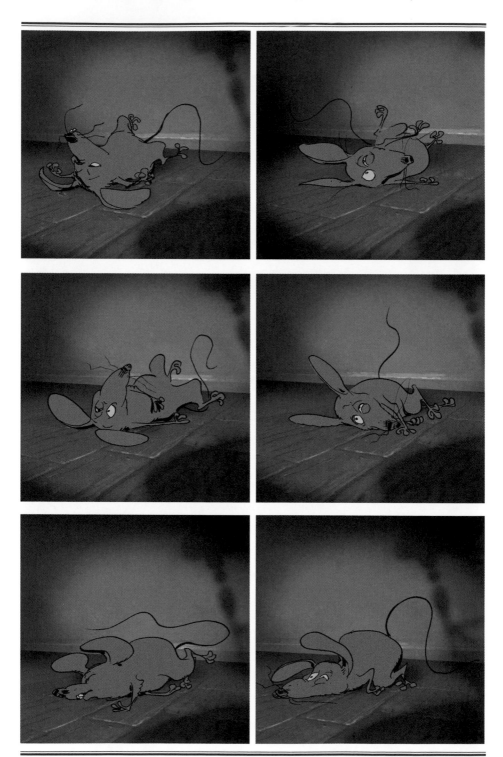

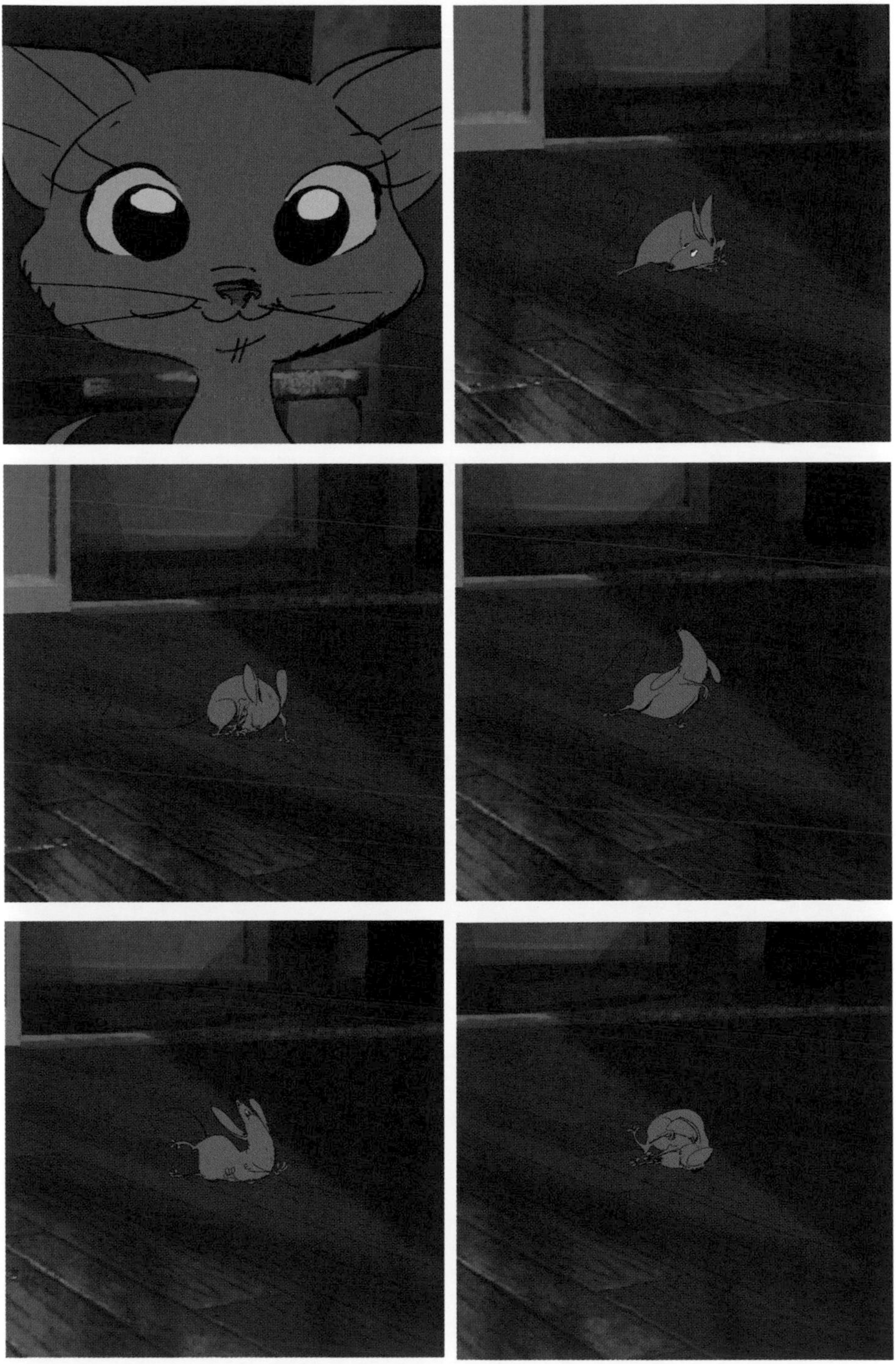

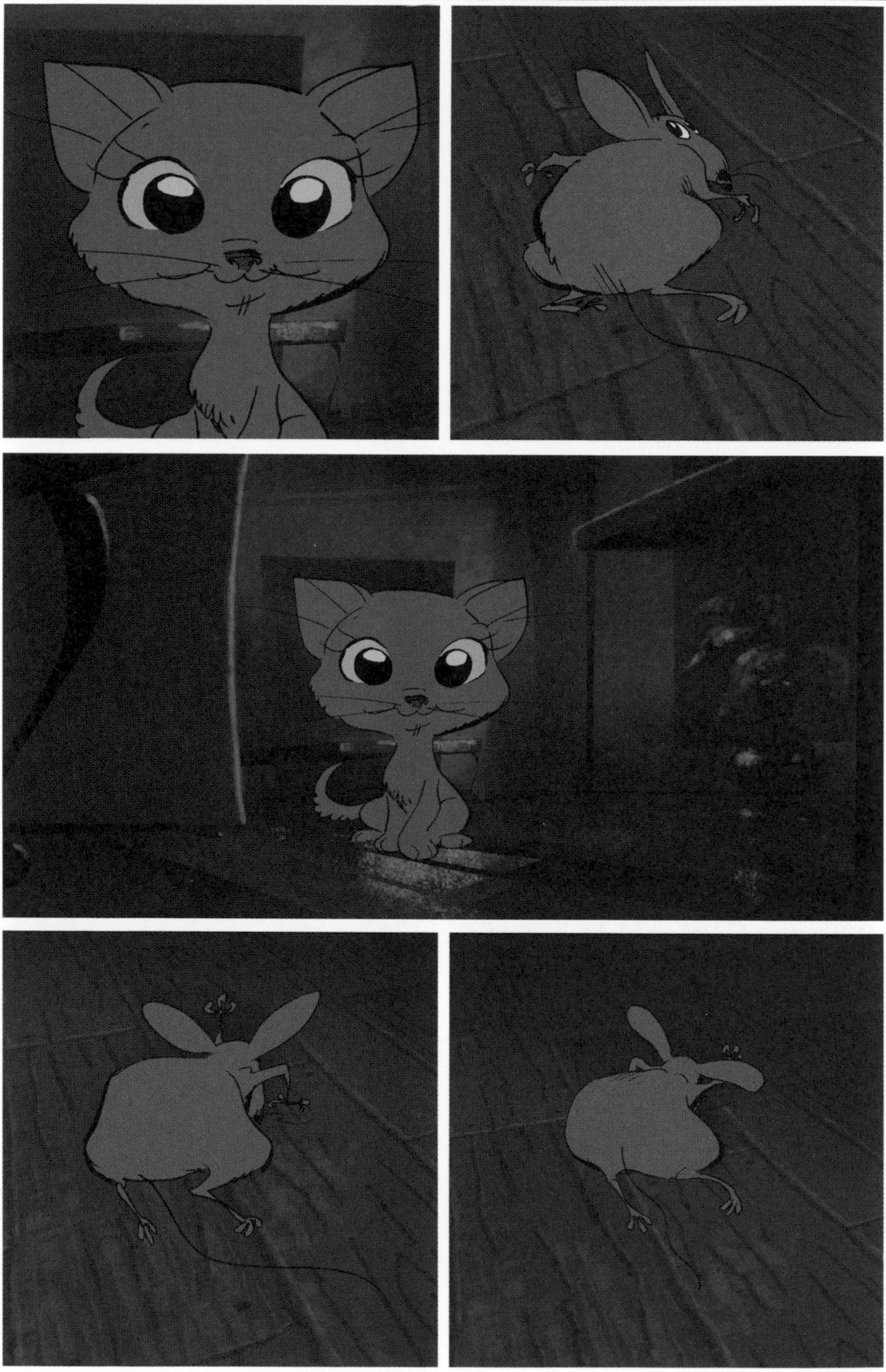

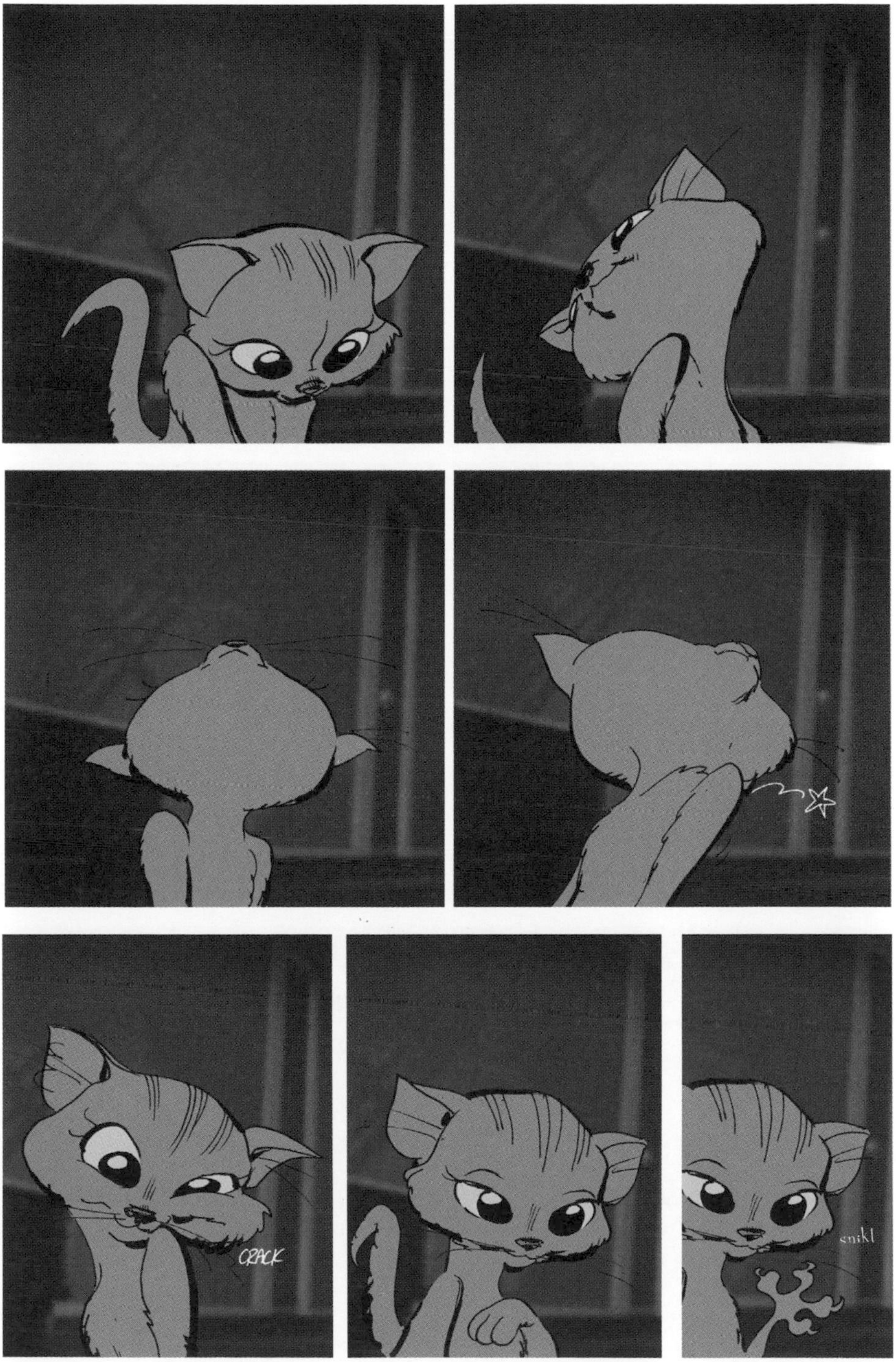
CRACK
snikl

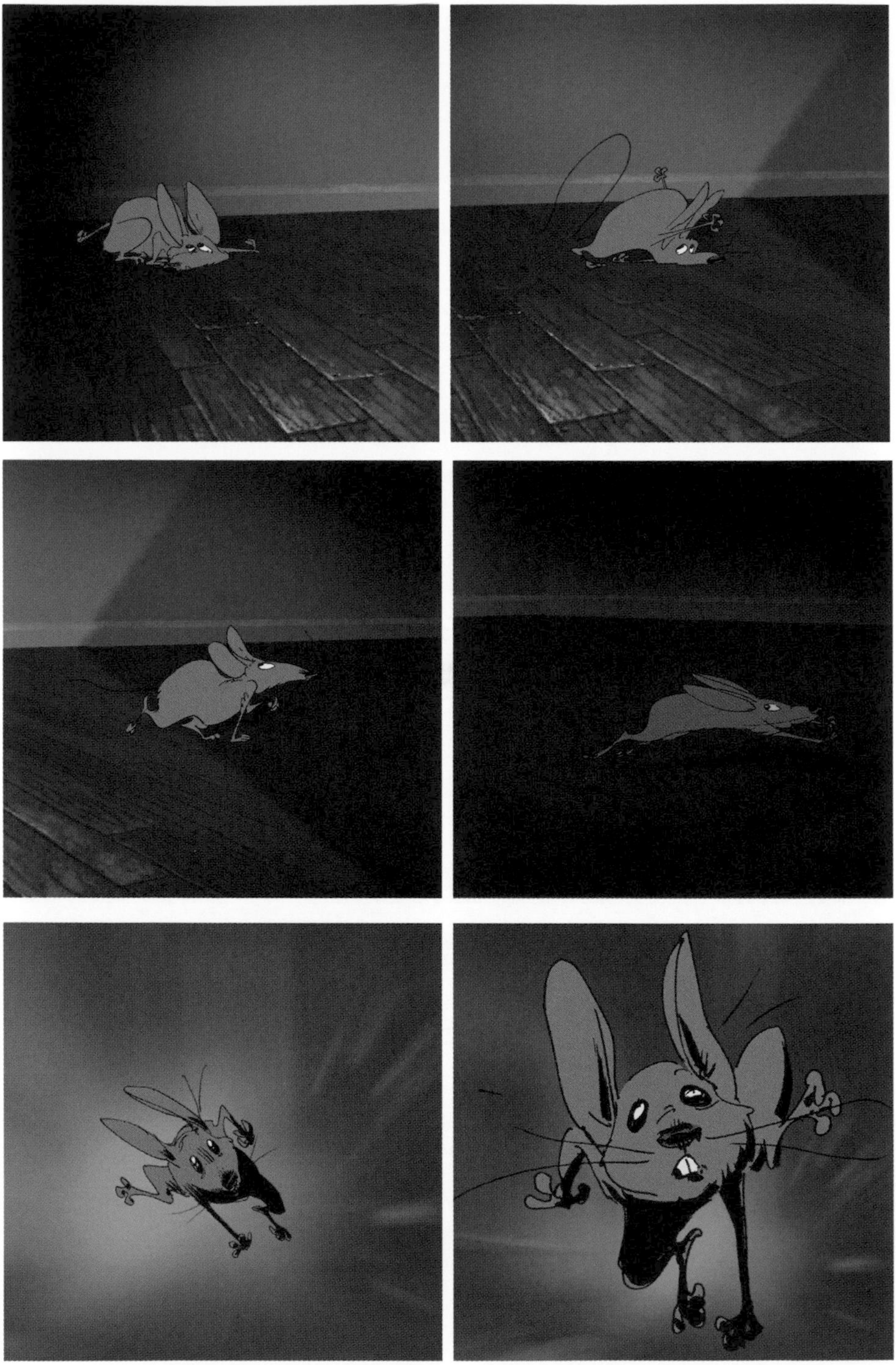

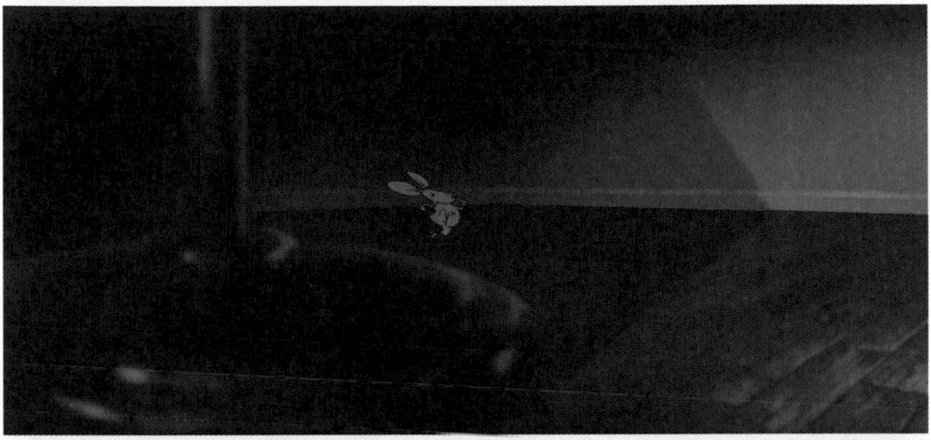

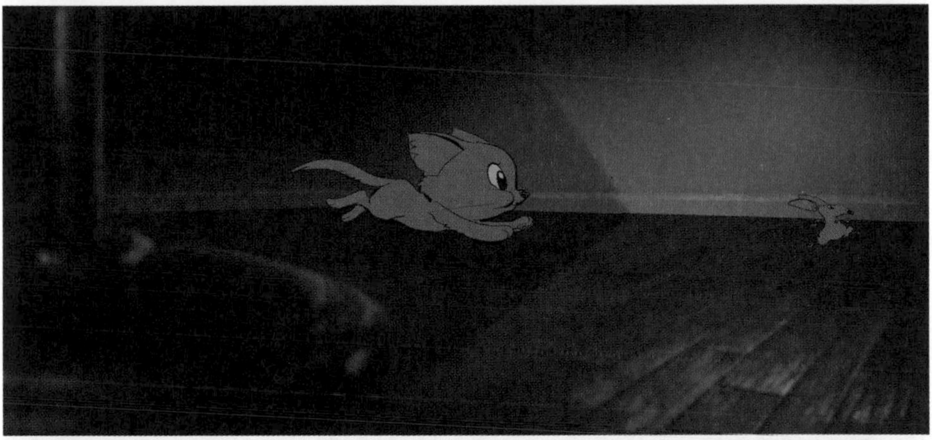

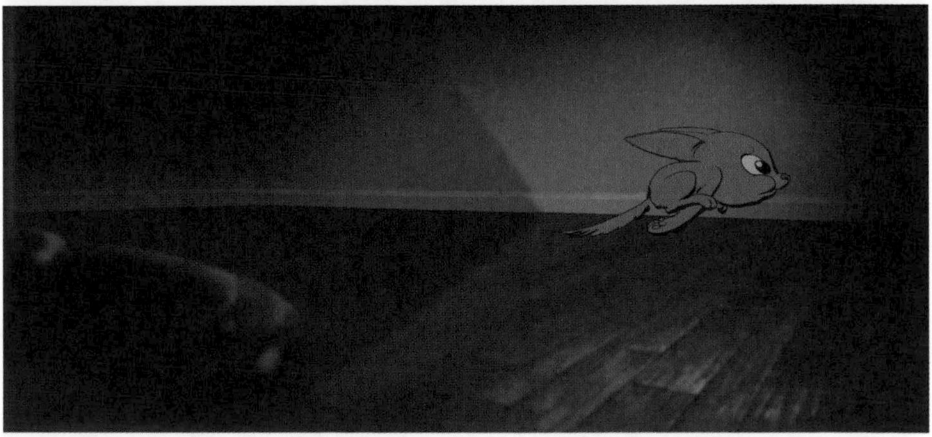

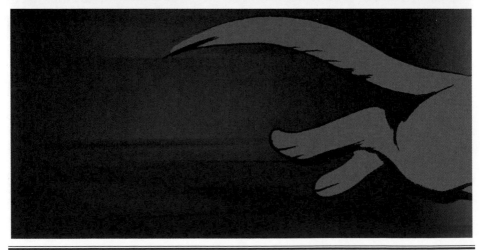

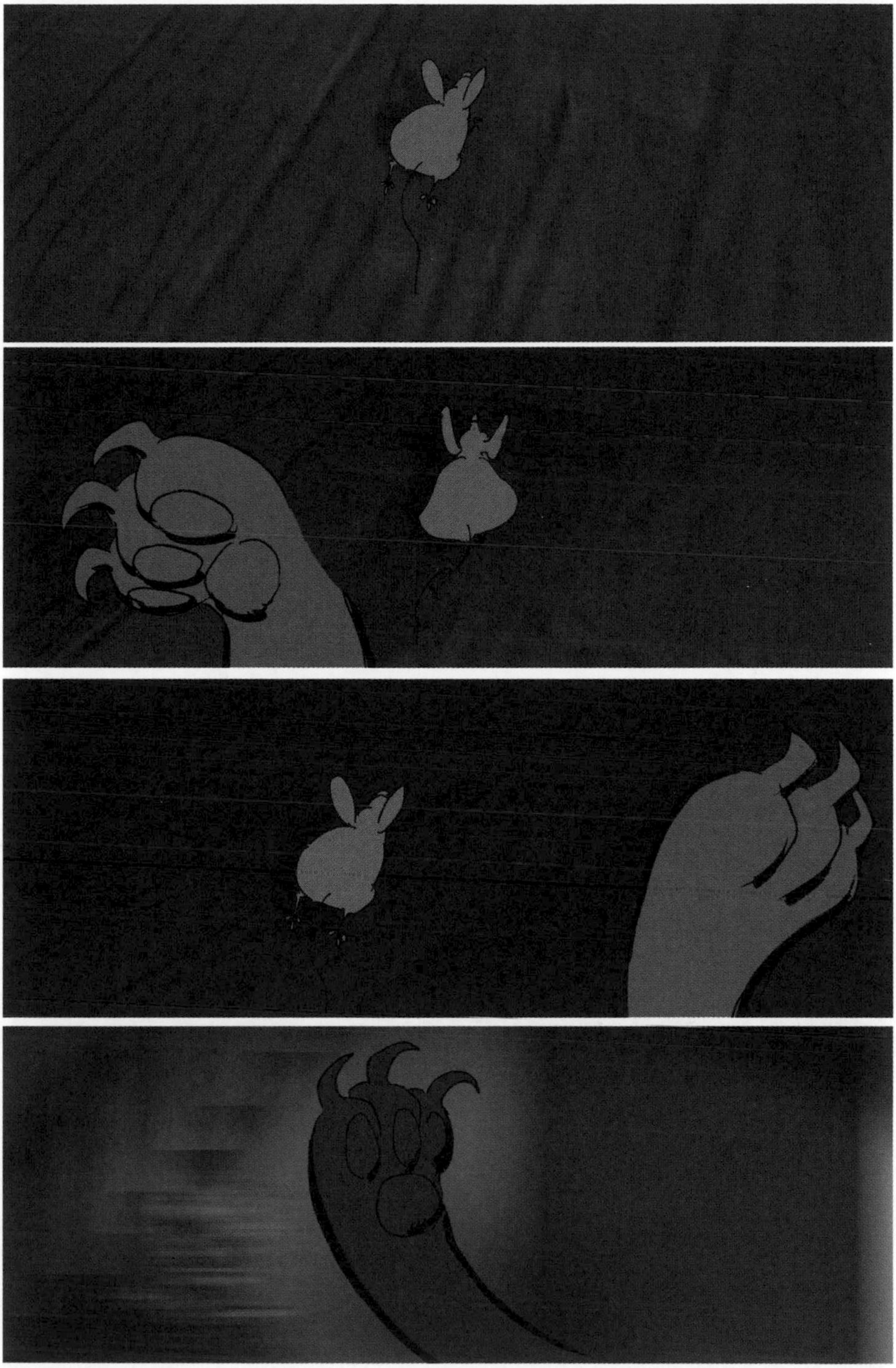

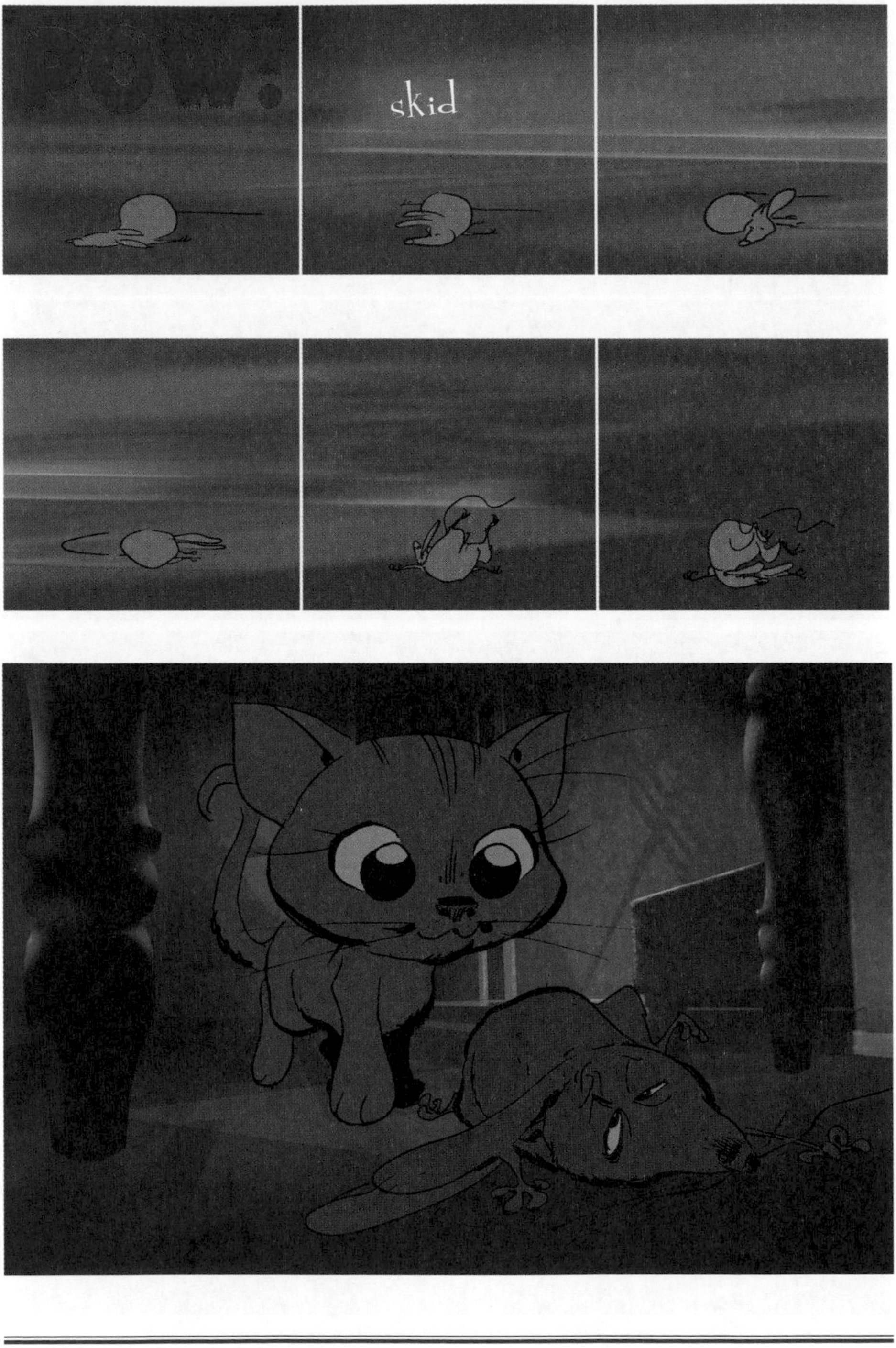
POW!
skid

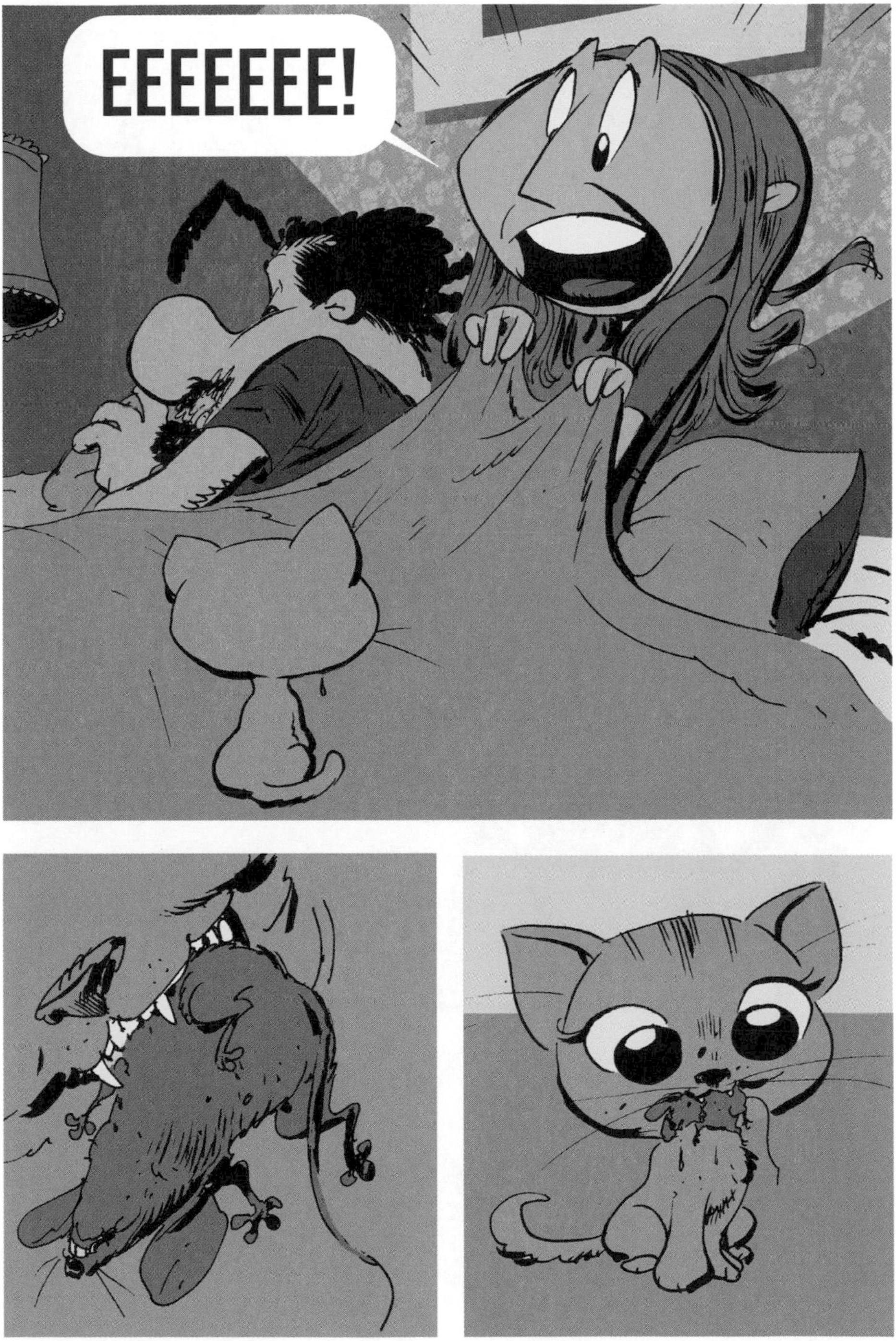
EEEEEEE!

Purr.
I was **going** to tell you.

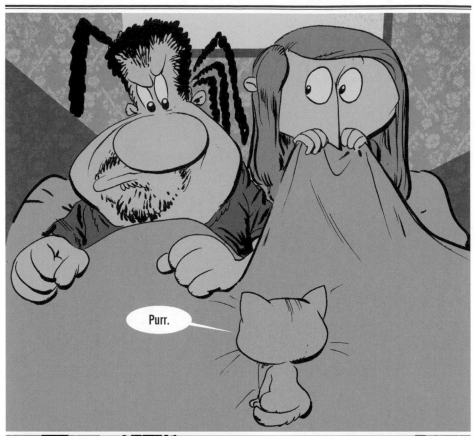

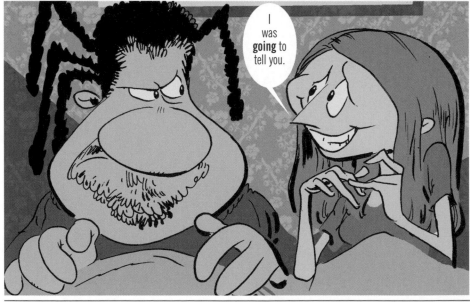

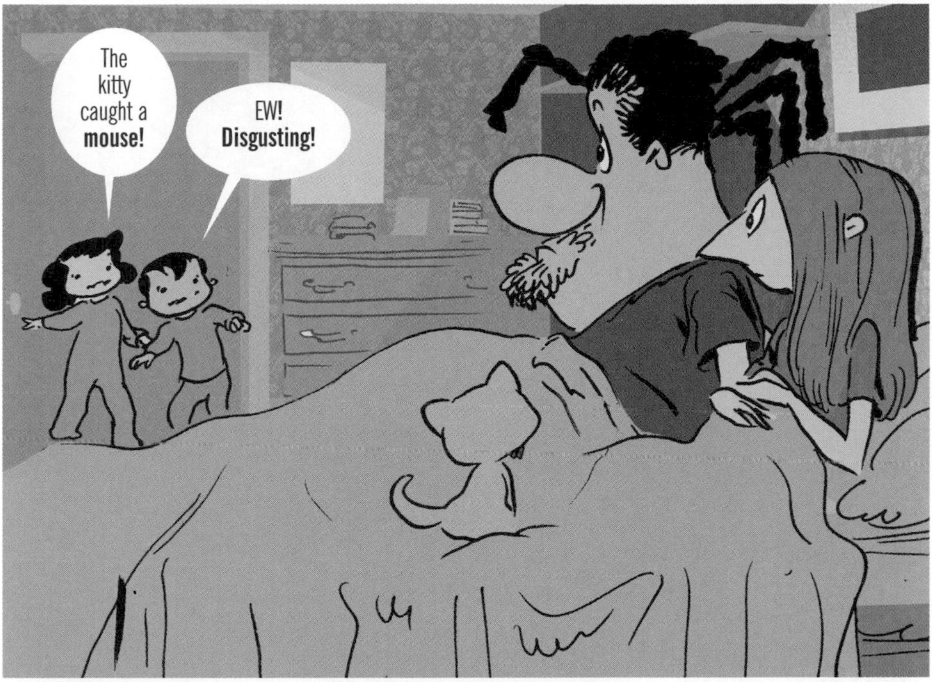
The kitty caught a **mouse!**
EW! **Disgusting!**

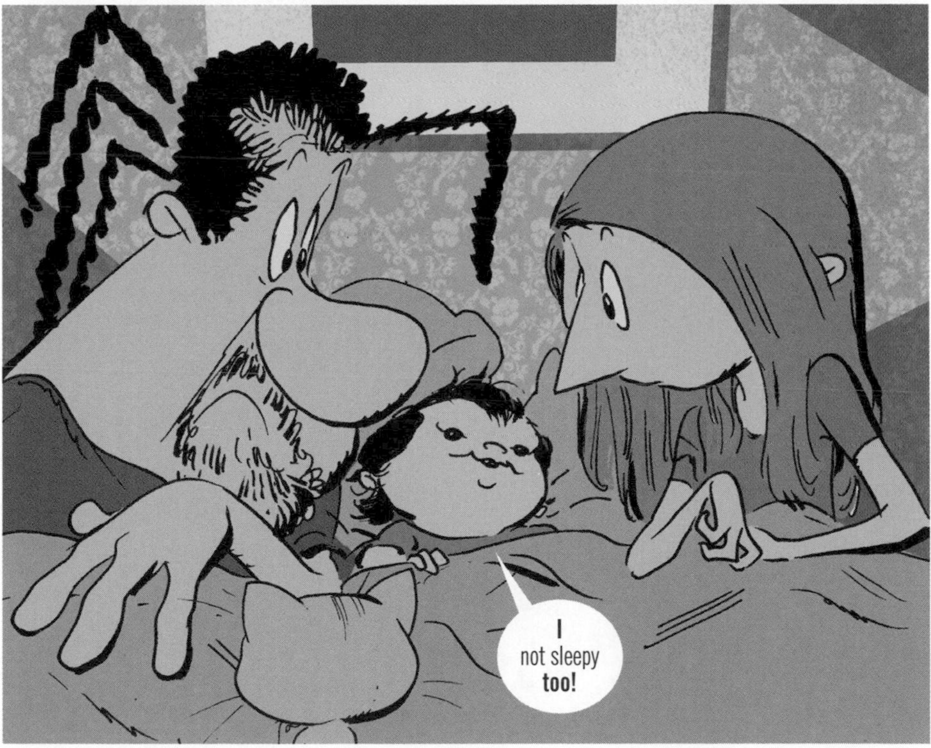
I not sleepy **too!**

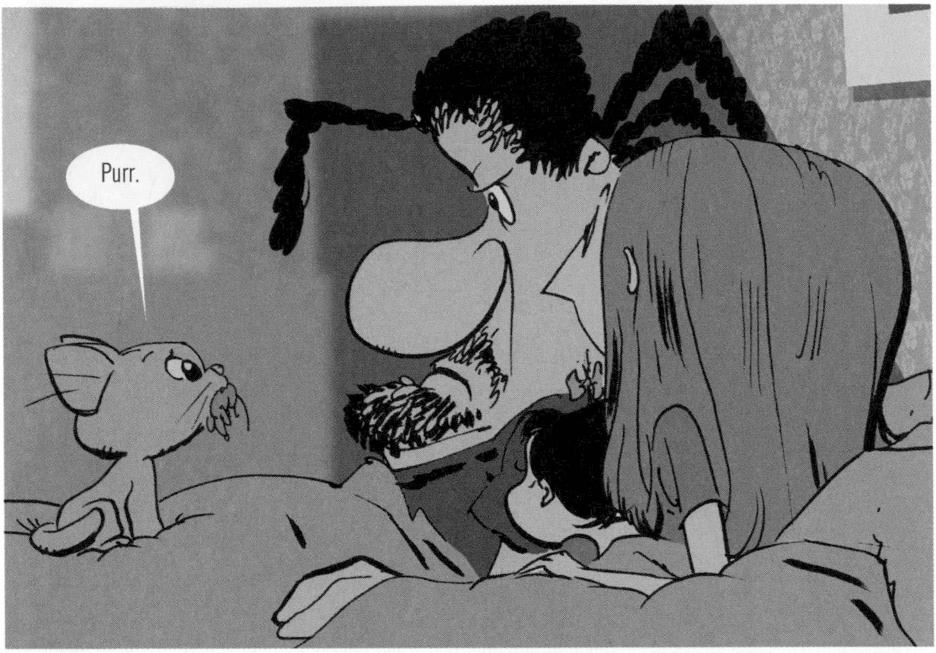
Purr.

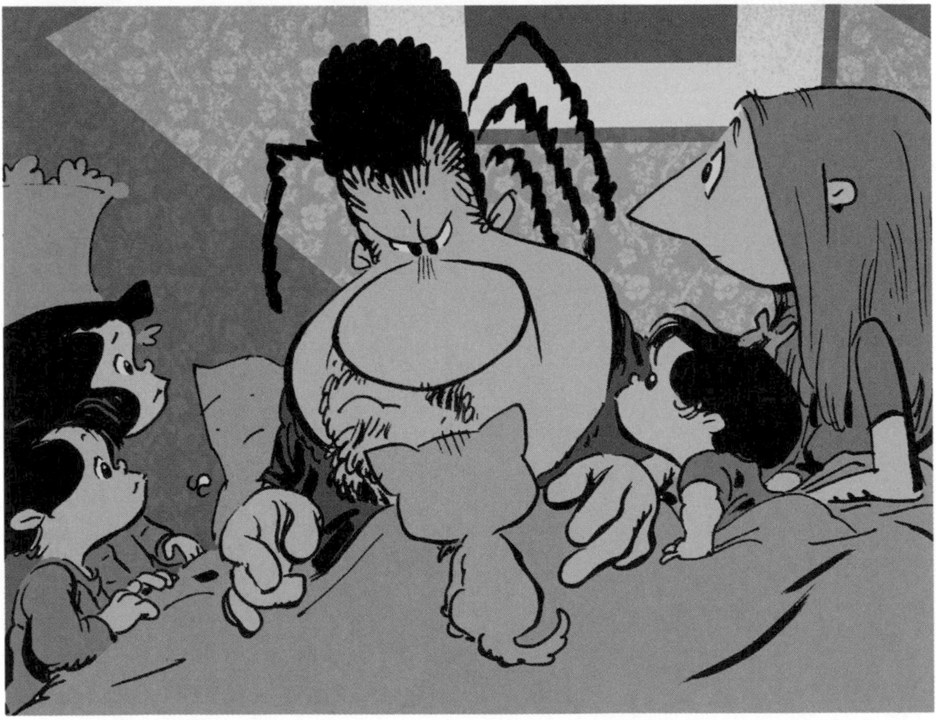

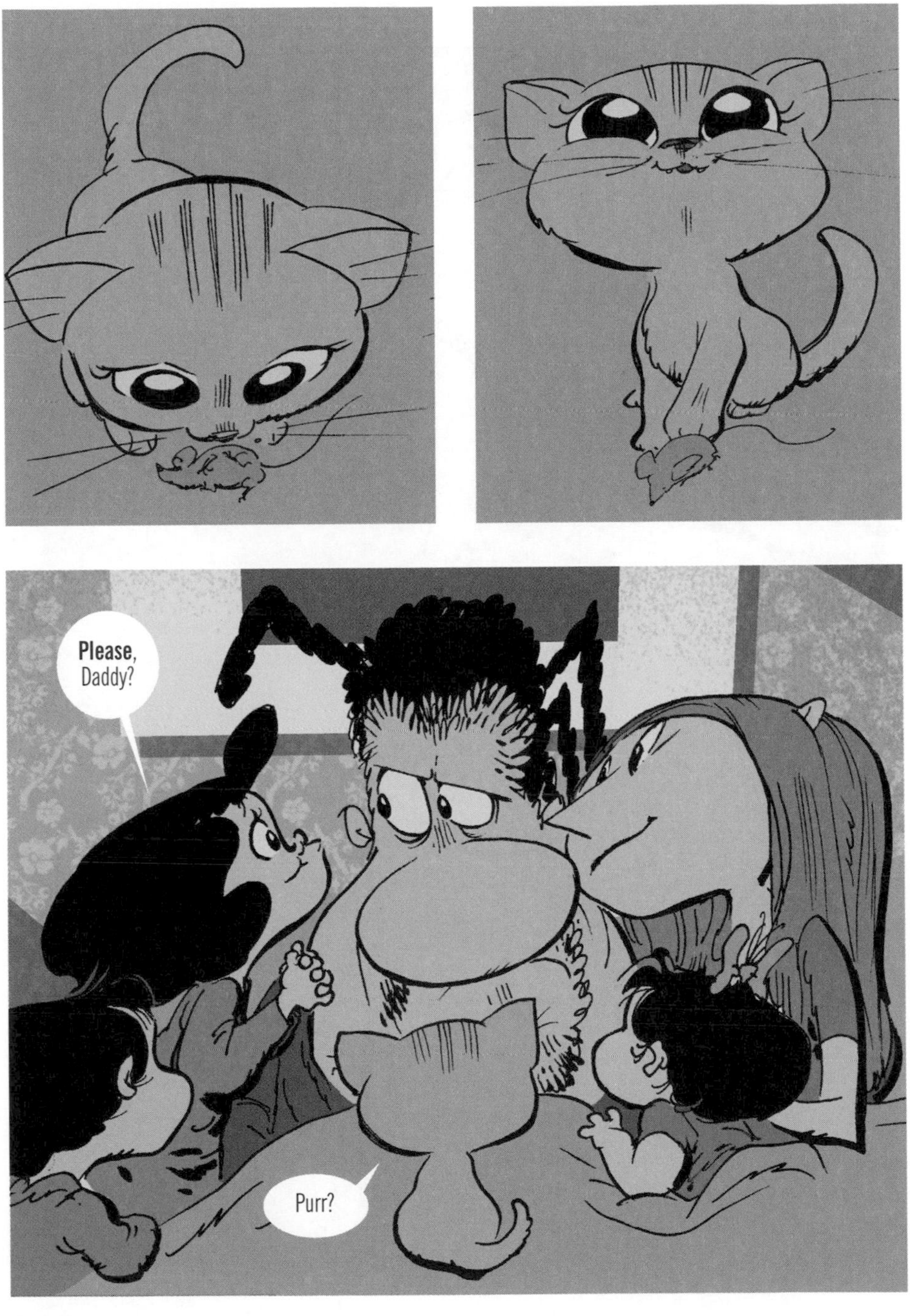
Please, Daddy?
Purr?

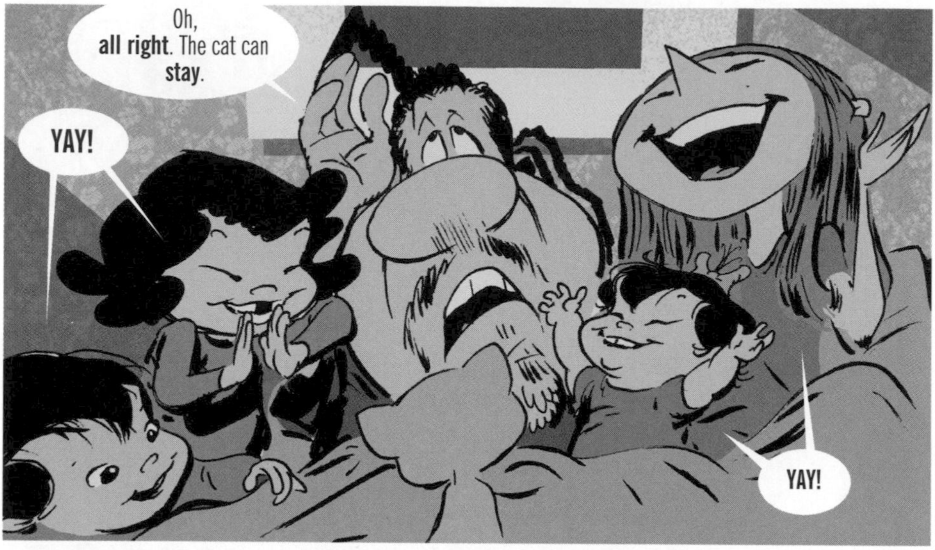
Oh,
all right. The cat can **stay**.
YAY!
YAY!

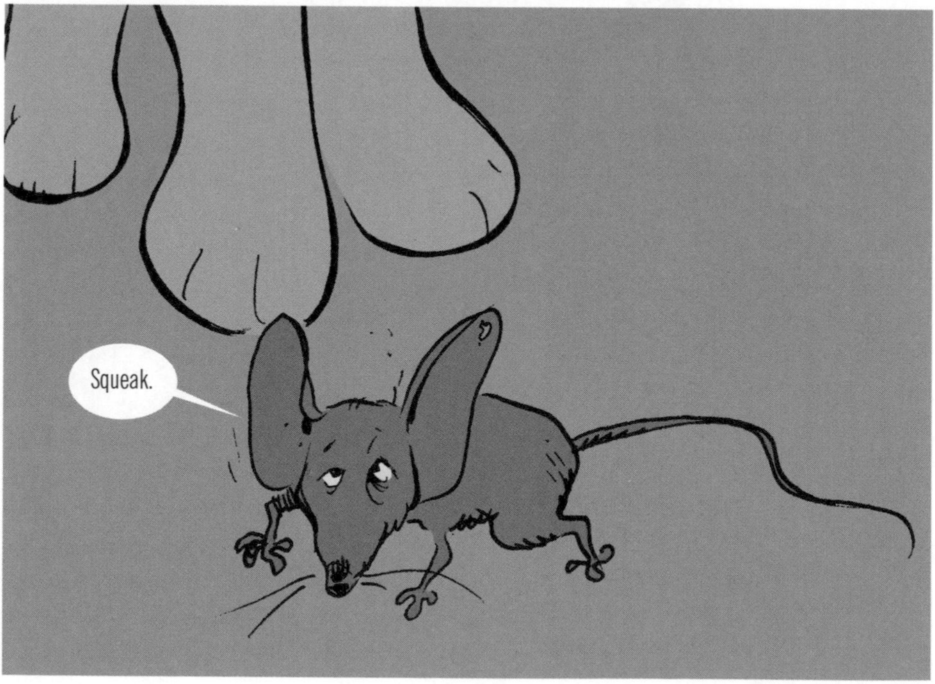
Squeak.

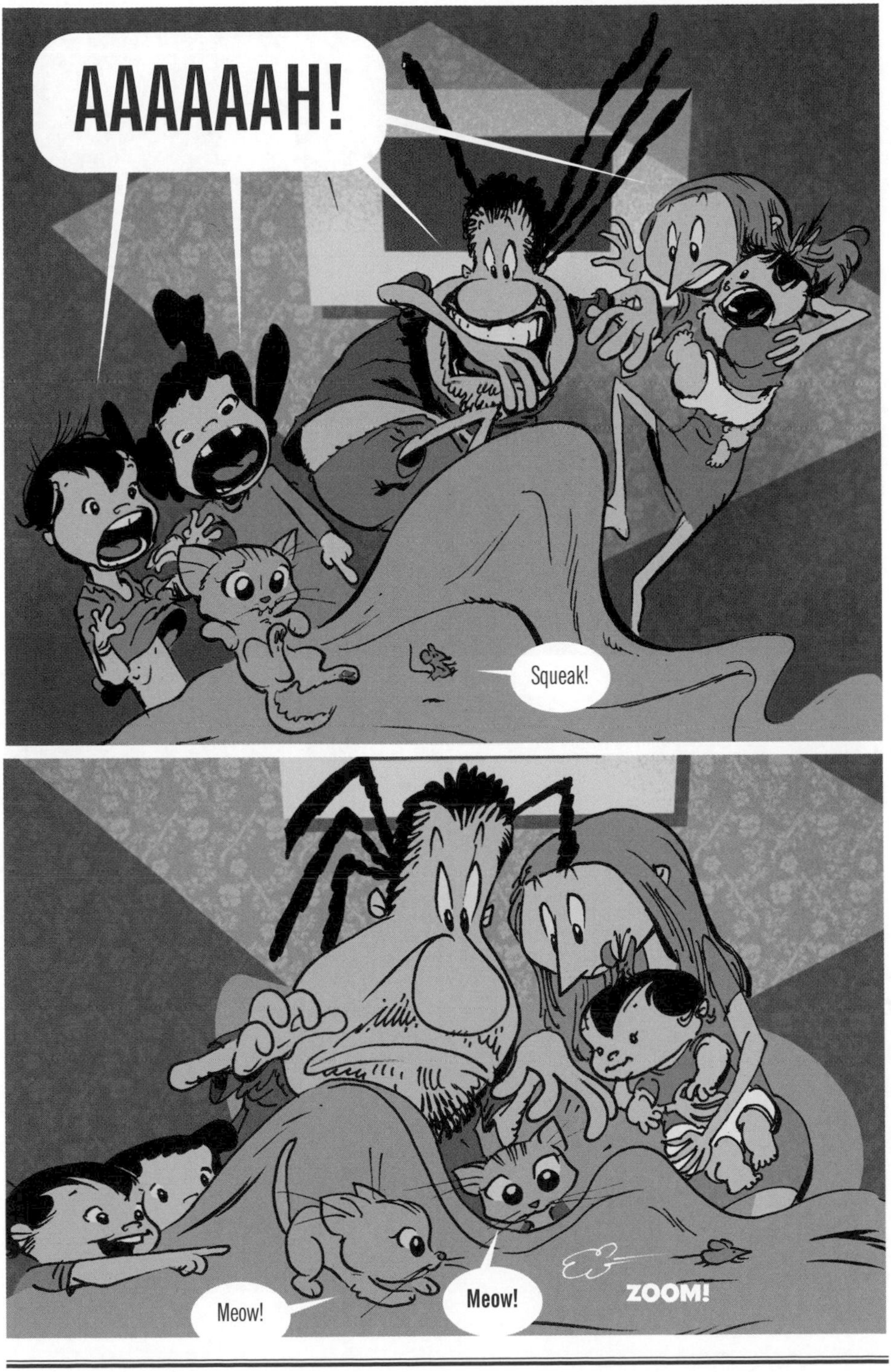
AAAAAAH!
Squeak!
Meow!
Meow!
ZOOM!

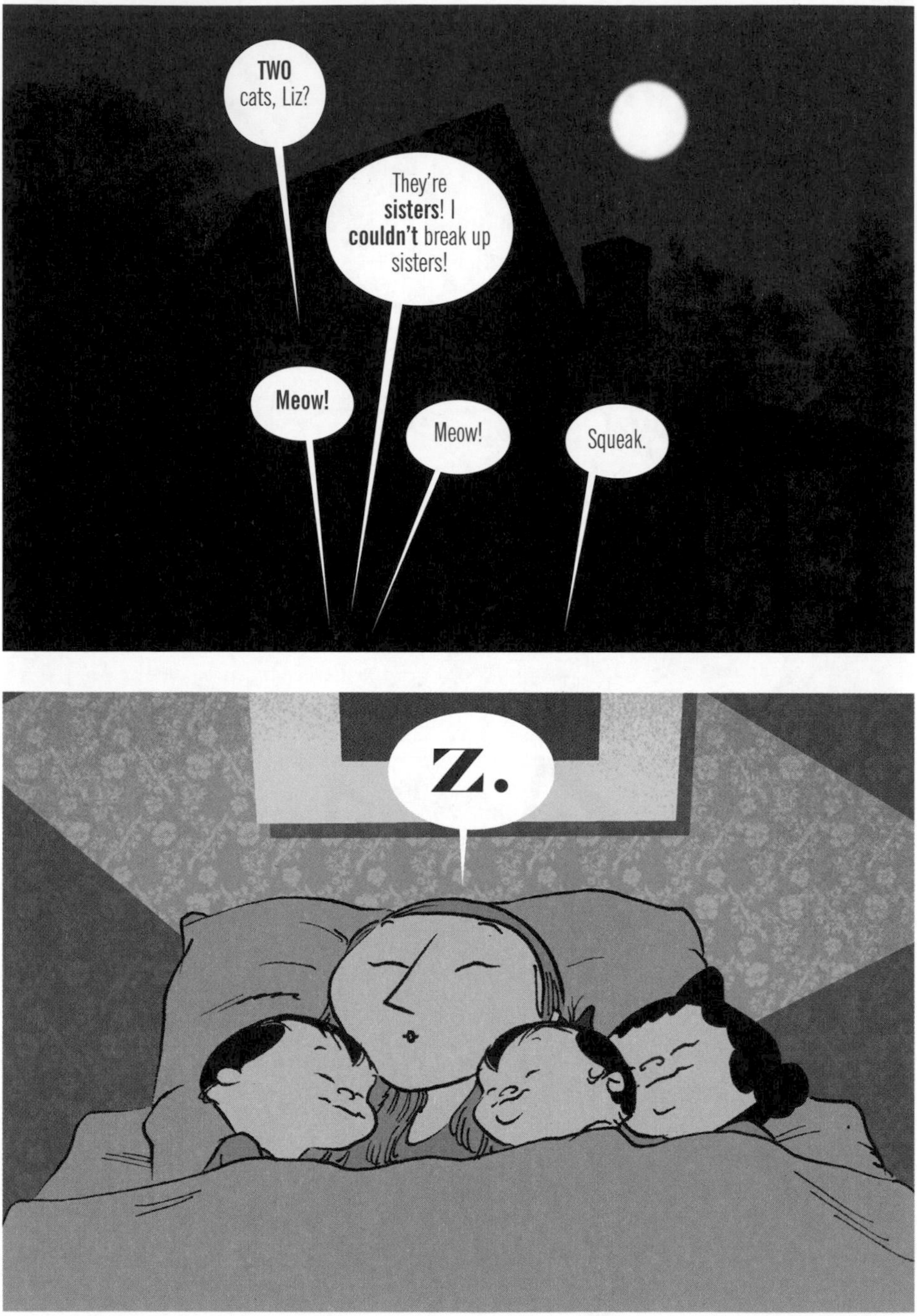

TWO cats, Liz?
They're sisters! I couldn't break up sisters!
Meow!
Meow!
Squeak.
Z.

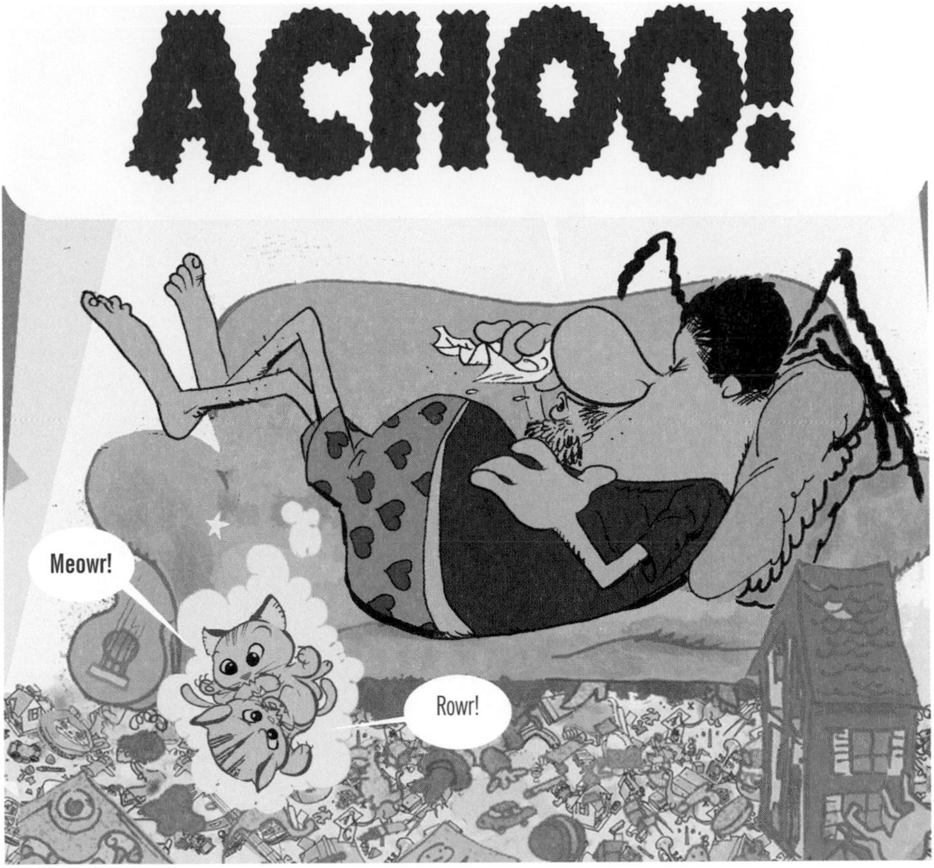
ACHOO!
Meowr!
Rowr!

THE END

A KYLE BAKER CARTOON

SKETCHBOOK

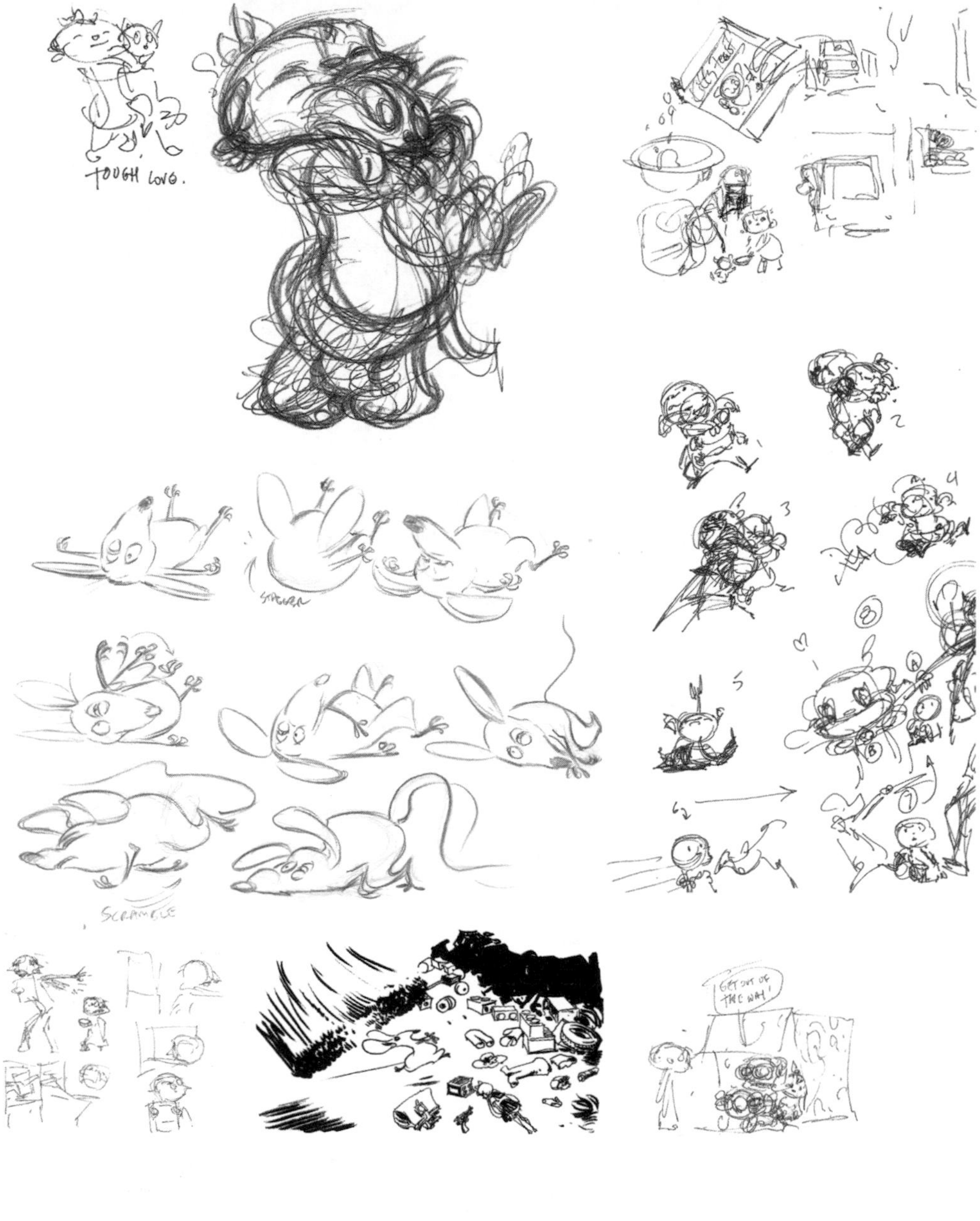
TOUGH LOVE.
SCRAMBLE
GET OUT OF THE WAY!

Visit WWW.KYLEBAKER.COM to see ANIMATED CARTOONS of The BAKERS and other characters. Download them! Share Them! Read new Bakers comics online! E-mail Kyle, become his Myspace friend, see interviews and EXCLUSIVE previews of upcoming Kyle Baker cartoons!

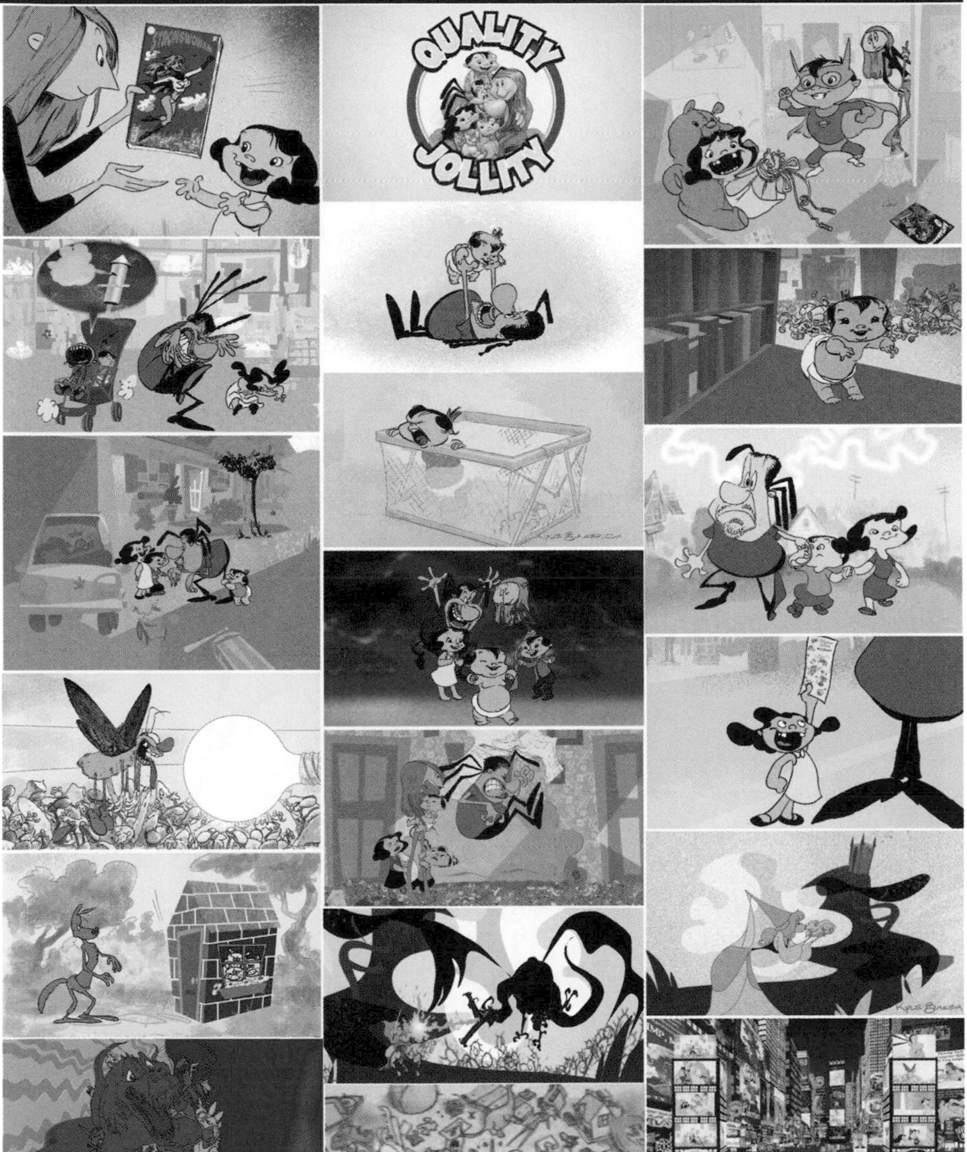

QUALITY
JOLLITY

If you enjoyed this book, you'll also love:

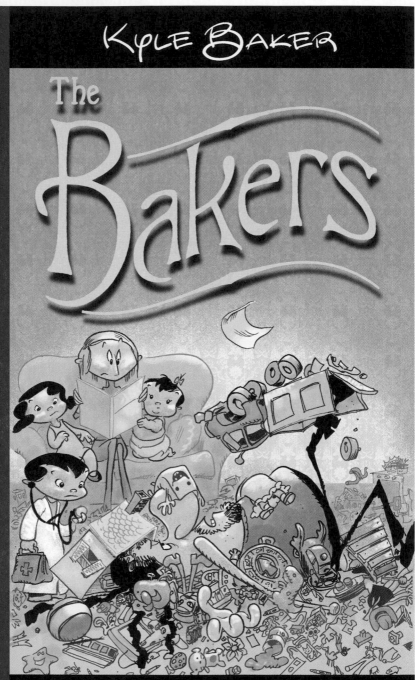

KYLE BAKER
The BaKers

"DO THESE TOYS BELONG SOMEWHERE?"

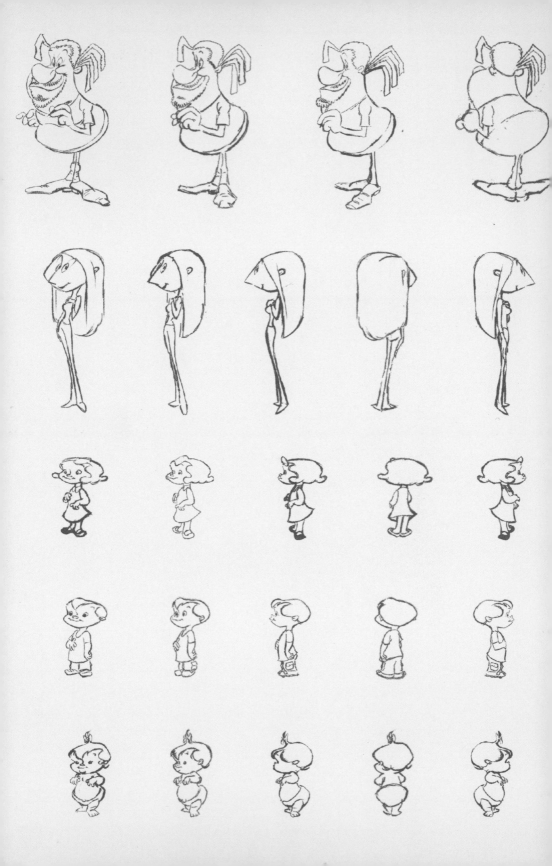